The End of
Mandatory Retirement

THE AUTHORS—James W. Walker is a consultant in human resource
planning, associated with Towers, Perrin, Forster & Crosby, New York.
From 1971 to 1978 he was responsible for the firm's consulting activities in human resource planning and development. He has worked
with more than 100 corporations and governmental organizations. He
is President of the Human Resource Planning Society, an association
of human resource specialists from 300 corporations. He is also a
member of the Gerontological Society and serves on the editorial
board of the journal Aging and Work, published by the National Council on the Aging. During his career Dr. Walker has also served on the
business faculties at Indiana University and San Diego State University.
He is currently on the business administration faculty of Arizona State
University. Harriet L. Lazer is a consultant with the communications
consulting firm of Brecker and Merryman, Inc. in New York. Her
specializations are career communications, career path analysis, and
recruitment programs. Her experience includes consulting assignments
with Union Carbide, Federated Department Stores, Macy's, AT&T,
and American Can Company. She is a graduate of Barnard College,
Columbia University.

JAMES W. WALKER

HARRIET L. LAZER

THE END OF MANDATORY RETIREMENT

Implications for Management

JOHN WILEY & SONS

New York · Chichester
Brisbane · Toronto

Library of Congress Cataloging in Publication Data:

Walker, James W.   1941-
    The end of mandatory retirement.

    "A Wiley-Interscience publication."
    Includes bibliographical references and index.
    1. Aged—Employment—United States.
2. Retirement, Mandatory—United States. 3. Personnel
management—United States. I. Lazer, Harriet L.,
joint author. II. Title.

HF5549.5.O44W34   658.31'3'2   78-13692
ISBN 0-471-04417-2

Printed in the United States of America

10 9 8 7 6 5 4 3 2 1

PREFACE

By sanctioning mandatory retirement we in-
advertently perpetuate the stereotype that
to be old is to be feeble-minded and
worthless—The Honorable Claude Pepper

The fight waged against age-65 mandatory retirement has
been victorious. Effective January 1, 1979, it will be generally illegal to force retirement or otherwise discriminate
in employment for individuals aged 40 through 69. As Representative Pepper noted, "the practice of age-based mandatory retirement is arbitrary and unwarranted. It is as
odious as discrimination based on race and sex." His sponsor-
ship of H.R. 5383, the act that ultimately became law, was a
potent force on Capitol Hill. Pepper as you may know, is 78
years old and not about to retire.

The new federal law does not, however, mandate that all
employees work until the age of 70. Pepper noted, "In no
way should the end of involuntary retirement because of age
be considered an attempt to limit an individual's right to opt
for early retirement if she or he so chooses. The right of an
older worker who is willing and able to work to continue
working regardless of age is not one that can or must be
traded for the right to retire voluntarily" (Select Committee
on Aging, 1977).

The laws and the changes they introduce will require modifications in management policies and practices. Pension and other retirement income plans will need some modification, but the major implications for change will occur in the administration of basic personnel systems in companies. Flexible retirement policies and practices designed to induce early retirements will have to be introduced. More effective administration of appraisal systems, particularly as they affect employment opportunities of older individuals, will have to be achieved. Job design, salary administration, career guidance, and other management practices will also be subject to modification.

The end of mandatory retirement may mean harsher treatment of some older employees whose performance levels are falling. For example, Malcolm Forbes (Editor of *Forbes*) observed in an editorial, that "Wiping out mandatory retirement at 65 is going to be very tough on some of the older people it is supposed to benefit. There are an appreciable, if statistically unascertainable, number of older employees who would have been fired but are kept on only because they are nearing retirement age. If it becomes illegal to have corporate mandatory retirement provisions at the age of 65, you can bet your boots that when one or another worker reaches mid-50s, a company will begin thinking about whether his or her services are going to be up to par for the next 20 years or so."

In a broader sense, the change is a significant shift in management philosophy mandated by federal law. No longer are loyalty and long service to be automatically rewarded. Employees are to be judged solely on merit and competence. This means that "Old Joe" will no longer be allowed to mellow on the job and step aside when "it is time to retire." Unless companies wish to terminate individuals for *cause*, they may have to tolerate them indefinitely. The law will essentially repeal the tenure tradition in American business.

To a considerable extent, the applications of the legislation will involve management efforts to make existing personnel systems work better rather than the introduction of wholly new systems. Protection of workers against age discrimination requires consistent, fair, and objective treatment in the terms and conditions of employment. The onus is on management's exercise of authority in making employment decisions affecting older employees. Subjectivity will be replaced by greater objectivity; informality will be replaced by more formal and documented actions. Systems now in place but loosely applied will be more rigorously administered.

With changes in practices we may also expect a shift in management attitudes toward aging and retirement. Because retirement will no longer be an automatic occurrence, managers will need to take individual motivations and differences into account to induce retirements. Treatment of employees will need to reflect an understanding of the facts of aging as they affect performance and competencies, as well as an appreciation of the legal constraints on age discrimination.

This book provides a concise review and analysis of the facts, issues, concepts, and managerial practices under a policy of flexible rather than mandatory retirement. The 1978 amendments to the Age Discrimination in Employment Act portend further federal legislation which will ban discrimination at any age and which will mandate improved benefit and compensation coverage for older employees. In the meantime, comprehensive age laws in California, Connecticut, and other states will become the norm guiding corporate personnel policies and practices. Flexible retirement is, therefore, an appropriate concern of management and an appropriate focus for this book.

In Part I the first three chapters offer an historical perspective of retirement practices and legislation, a synopsis of demographic and social factors, and an overview of the federal and state laws affecting management practices. The aging of our population and our work force is a major factor impelling changes in retirement law. Not only the sheer numbers but the attitudes and life styles represented among older workers in our society must be understood by managers.

Part II of the book then considers the management strategies necessary for an effective response to these legal and demographic conditions. Flexible retirement practices, early retirement programs and related retirement inducements, and strategies for controlling benefit and other personnel costs for older employees are discussed.

Part III examines the management steps necessary to define job requirements that are free of age bias as criteria for employee selection, training, and compensation. Courts have given preliminary guidance regarding what constitutes valid performance appraisals and job standards, and these guidelines are examined in the context of practical management needs for appraisals.

Part IV reviews pertinent facts, concepts, and theories from the fields of gerontology, psychology, sociology, and geriatrics to answer the question: What should managers know about the facts of aging? Both biological and psychological aspects are discussed, along with an analysis of why employees decide to retire when they do and how they go about adjusting to retirement.

In Part V guidance is offered regarding ways of studying employee feelings about retirement and career plans. Through effective two-way communications with employees, retirement preparation and counseling may be tailored to fit the particular interests and needs prevailing among older employees.

Part VI provides a guide to the literature available to managers regarding the many interrelated aspects of this complex field. The most significant references are highlighted.

The central objective of this book, then, is to aid management in responding to the practical challenges imposed by the coming end of mandatory retirement and associated prohibitions against employment discrimination based on age. Flexible retirement, an alternative to rigid practices existing in many companies, can be introduced and effectively managed. Given the legal, social, and pragmatic business demands converging today, it is the only alternative.

We gratefully acknowledge the substantive contributions to this book by the staff of TPF&C. We are indebted also to our co-researchers on retirement attitudes, Karl Price, Doug Kimmel, and Howard Risher. Finally, appreciation is due to those individuals who have stimulated our interest in the subject of retirement and have guided our research and thinking on this subject, including Gordon Streib, Nancy Peavy, Michael Batten, Sara Rix, and Harold Sheppard.

JAMES W. WALKER
HARRIET L. LAZER

Tempe, Arizona
July 1978

CONTENTS

PART ONE
BACKGROUND

CHAPTER ONE

RETIREMENT: A REDEFINITION

What Congress is now considering is an act of social policy, not constitutional rights—Editorial, *New York Times,* October 21, 1977, p. A40.

Social change comes slowly, particularly change in long-established social patterns such as retirement timing. But however slowly, change does occur, and a major change in our definition of retirement has materialized. Attitudes of Americans toward retirement, toward old age, and toward working careers have changed over generations, reflecting prevailing social and economic conditions. The most recent manifestation of our social attitudes in this area is the enactment of federal and state laws prohibiting or modifying mandatory retirement practices of employers.

Changing conditions give rise to changing attitudes, which give rise to new laws, representing de facto social policy. These parameters of management policy and practice, in turn, affect the actual work and retirement patterns of individuals in our society. New laws are recognition that our attitudes toward the aging are changing. They impel management to acknowledge these changing attitudes and, further, to understand what is going on and to adjust policies and practices in response.

HISTORICAL ATTITUDES TOWARD AGING

Attitudes toward aging (and therefore toward older persons) have changed over the centuries in accordance with demographic, economic, social, and political circumstances. In colonial America, for example, there were very few older people, but they held a lot of authority (Fischer, 1977). At that time only one out of five persons lived to be 70 years old, compared with four out of five today.

In early American meeting houses, the seats of highest honor and authority went to the oldest persons. Younger people had little to say about this, as older people controlled the land and the government. Religious beliefs reinforced the value of respect for one's elders. As a result, young people were sometimes exploited, bullied, and, often, ignored.

As social historian David Hackett Fischer notes, "Elderly people rarely retired to make way for the young. Old men worked until they wore out. Public leaders clung to office until death removed them—90 per cent of New England's ministers and magistrates died in office." That society's officials ruled with the authority of age is reflected in their titles: elder, alderman, senator. But Fischer also notes that there were also poor old men who suffered as paupers and there were some elderly who were resented and despised because of their authority. Although old age was exalted by law and custom, it was often resented because of association with power, arrogance, cruelty, and greed.

It was because of the exalted power of aged that people often tried to look older by powdering their hair and wearing clothes that imitated fashions of older people. But with the American Revolution, the social status of the aged began to fall. Fashions reversed; new laws were passed forcing politicians to retire at a fixed age. The first such law passed in New York State in 1777—setting age limits for judges.

Between 1780 and 1820, established attitudes were disrupted. Some attribute changing attitudes to the Industrial Revolution, but in fact this had not yet had its effect (which occurred later, in the latter part of the nineteenth century). Virtually all Americans still lived in the country and were farmers. Rather, the driving force for change was another form of revolution: the social revolutions in America and France. The ideal of equality seemed to contradict the elite status of older persons in power. The drive for communal government knocked down not only political authorities but established status hierarchies and wealth structures as well.

In the nineteenth century the cult of youth, not age, was well established. As Thoreau noted in *Walden*, "I have yet to hear the first syllable of valuable or even earnest advice from my seniors. They have told me nothing, and probably cannot teach me anything." Harsh as it seems, youth became favored, and the aged became dependent.

As both the percentage of the population over age 65 and the percentage of these who were retired increased, attention turned to the unique needs of the aging. Aging became a "social problem." In 1909 the first Commission on Aging was appointed, in Massachusetts. Federal programs were proposed. Private pension plans were developed. Arizona established the first state pension system in 1915. Even new fields of study were born: geriatrics and gerontology.

ORIGINS OF MANDATORY RETIREMENT

Prior to the passage of the Social Security Act in 1935, mandatory retirement was rare. Employees retired when they were told to or worked until they were unable. Many died while working. In fact, an underlying intent of the Social Security Act and of many private pension programs was to provide assistance to older individuals who might not have the means of supporting themselves in their old age.

The age of 65 was incorporated in the federal legislation

as the minimum age of eligibility for benefits. Apparently, this age was adopted arbitrarily or at best considered to be a "normal" and acceptable age level to use. There was reportedly no discussion on the appropriateness of this age. The same age had previously been adopted in the social security system established in Germany, also apparently without rationale.

Since 1935, however, life expectancy has improved. More Americans are surviving to the age of 65 and more are retiring from their working careers. Also, more workers are employed by the government and by private employers, and fewer are working on farms. Employers have been less tolerant of the physical disabilities of the aged and have adopted formal policies governing retirement age.

Mandatory retirement has become commonplace in American business and government. Although many working Americans are not covered by such provisions because they are self-employed or work in professions where mandatory retirement has not been customary (law, medicine, dentistry, etc.), the concept of mandatory retirement is widely acknowledged. The age of 65, reinforced by Social Security provisions, has become regarded as the "normal time" to retire.

RETIREMENT AGE

At this point, a clarification of "retirement age" is appropriate. Mandatory retirement age generally refers to a personnel policy established by an employer that prohibits employment after a certain specified age, historically 65. Even under such a policy, exceptions are often made if certain individuals have knowledge or skills desired by the company. If not retained as employees, they are placed on consultant or part-time status.

Many employers also have a retirement age considered

"normal" under provisions of pension or other retirement benefit plans. At this age the employee is eligible to receive a full, unreduced retirement benefit. Beyond this age, no further accruals are made. This age for eligibility for unreduced benefits has been lowered by many companies, from 70 to 65, 62, or even 60 and lower, to induce early retirements. In some instances normal retirement age is determined by a combination of age and service in years (e.g., totaling 85).

Under the Age Discrimination in Employment Act of 1967 (ADEA), it is legal to observe the terms of a bona fide retirement benefit plan, as long as the plan was not a subterfuge of the purposes of the act. The Supreme Court interpreted this provision to mean that employees could be required to retire pursuant to a bona fide pension plan. The intricacies of this provision are discussed in Chapter 3, but they become moot with the 1978 amendments. Pension plans may continue to specify a normal retirement age, but the decision to retire must now be voluntary if it is before the age of 70.

WHEN DO EMPLOYEES RETIRE?

There is also a predominant retirement age in every organization: the age at which *most* employees retire. This may be considered the "normal age" among employees who tend to follow the example set by peers. Mandatory retirement policies and Social Security provisions made the age of 65 an "acceptable" age at which to retire. Over recent years, the predominant age has fallen to 62, as individuals have been attracted to early retirement and liberalized retirement income benefits provided.

Social Security statistics indicate that in 1956, when the law was amended to allow reduced benefits for women at age 62, only 2.2% of all benefit recipients accepted the reduced benefits available at early retirement. By 1974, 72% of all new awards were made to retired workers with reduced benefits. The law allows retirements as early as 60.

More people are planning early retirement than a decade ago. A 1976 survey by the University of Michigan's Survey Research Center revealed that 40% of working family heads from ages 35 to 63 planned to retire before the age of 65. One in four of those 35 to 59 years of age planned to retire before 62. Finances, including mortgage obligations, are a major consideration in retirement timing, along with responsibility for children and ability to continue working.

Statistics from both private and public sectors support the view that the trend is steadily toward early retirement. General Motors reported that the average age in 1975 for retirement was 58 and that only 2% of its workers remain until the mandatory retirement age. A 1977 Conference Board survey of executives said that over 50% of employees were retiring early. A survey of 28 companies conducted by Towers, Perrin, Forster & Crosby (TPF&C) found that executives are more likely to retire early than other employee groups, in part because they are financially able (TPF&C, 1974).

Of course, some early retirees are returning to work on other jobs and are thus in second careers and "double dipping" for income. This means they are receiving both retirement income benefits and current earned income. An often-cited example is an aide to H.E.W. Secretary Califano who is a federal retiree drawing a substantial pension in addition to his current (and also substantial) salary.

An aim of social change regarding mandatory retirement has been to foster employment of older persons—to enable individuals to work beyond the policy-mandated retirement age if they so desire. Neither pension plan provisions nor personnel policies should be used, according to advocates, as a basis for terminating an individual's career involuntarily. Nevertheless, experience suggests that relatively few employees will wish to prolong their working careers. Most employees voluntarily retire prior to the age of 65, and few wish to work beyond that age, let alone beyond the age of 70.

There are no general statistics to guide a company in estimating how many employees will stay on to the age of 65 or 70. As illustrated in the above citations, retirement timing varies with the employee group (e.g., hourly auto workers), attitudes, and company circumstances and benefits offered. Accordingly, a company needs to develop both its own experiential data and a profile of attrition of employees turning age 60. Such a profile is presented in Figure 1 and may be drawn to represent the actual experience of a company.

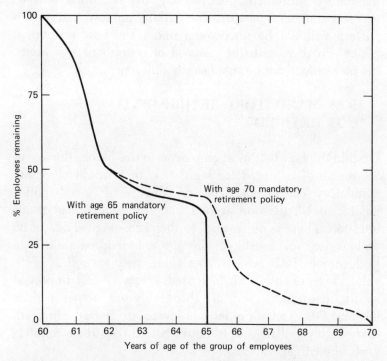

Figure 1. When Employees Retire: An Illustration of Retirement Timing for a Group of Employees at the Age of 60 and Over.

The solid line indicates the proportion of employees remaining each year for a group of employees who have turned 60 (a cohort group). In this example, half the employees had retired (or were terminated for cause, deceased, or disabled) within 2 years, when the group reached the age of 62. By the age of 65 about one-fourth of the group remained employed by the company, but because of the mandatory retirement policy, all were gone before any employee reached 66. (Typically, a policy requires that an employee retire on January 1 closest to his or her 65th birthday).

Also shown in this example by the dotted line is the possible pattern of continued employment under an age-70 mandatory retirement policy. Only 15% remained past 65 and few remained past 67. The authors propose that such a pattern will not be uncommon under the new retirement policy. Further, with the removal of retirement age limits, the pattern will not be significantly different.

HOW MANDATORY RETIREMENT "GOT RETIRED"

Despite the fact that most employees retire before the age of 65, pressures mounted for legislation that would eliminate mandatory retirement. The proponents of social policy change and legislation argued that this is a human rights question. There is no "magic" to the chronological age of 65 and no clear relationship of this age to individual abilities to perform jobs satisfactorily. Age alone, they argued, is not a valid determinant. With increased longevity and improved health, many individuals are still highly productive in their 60s and 70s. Today's older employees are better educated, more highly skilled, and in better health than their counterparts of past generations.

As a result, federal legislation did not evolve without controversy. Although the forces for change strongly prevailed in Congress, as reflected in the final votes of passage, the pros and cons of mandatory retirement were widely voiced. In fact, the forces opposing the legislation were acknowledged through several modifications in the legislation originally proposed.

A summary of the arguments raised for and against the proposed legislation in House of Representatives hearings is presented in Figure 2. A comparison of the positions suggests that the ultimate effects of the legislation cannot be predicted; only actual experience will demonstrate the validity of the assumptions represented. The absence of a factual basis for assessing argumentative positions was a serious limitation in the consideration of the legislation. Studies and published articles tended to be hortatory and were repetitious. The legislation passed through both houses so quickly, in fact, that there was little time to research the claims made by either side. The issue became one of righting an "obvious moral wrong," and the legislation a political necessity in view of a widespread public sentiment in its favor.

Nevertheless, many companies expressed concern about the difficulty of applying a flexible retirement policy evenhandedly. Spokesmen for Exxon, General Motors, and CBS argued, in opposition to legislation, that mandatory retirement programs protect workers against unequal treatment. Mandatory retirement provides a predictable situation for management and employees, favoring administrative simplicity. A limit on tenure based on age makes it easier for companies to remove less qualified personnel, allows prediction of pension and other benefit costs, and avoids disputes with employees with regard to termination of employment at age 65 and beyond.

On the other hand, the American Medical Association, in opposing mandatory retirement at any age, observed that the sudden shock of compulsory retirement and loss of earning power and productive work often leads to physical and

For Mandatory Retirement	Against Mandatory Retirement
1. A single policy dictating retirement at a set age protects employees against unequal treatment by avoiding the pitfalls of individual-merit judgments.	Mandatory retirement based on age alone is contrary to equal employment opportunity. It denies individuals equal protection of the law.
2. As a group, older persons are less well-suited for some jobs than younger workers because of declining physical and mental capacity, inflexibility, and less education.	Chronological age alone as a basis for mandatory retirement does not take into consideration actual, differing abilities and capacities. Studies demonstrate that many employees can continue to perform effectively beyond age 65 and may be better employees because of experience and job commitment.
3. Mandatory retirement saves face for the older worker no longer capable of performing, one who would otherwise be singled out for forced retirement.	Mandatory retirement has proven in many cases to result in impaired health and mental well-being to many capable of working adequately.
4. Older workers can often retire to Social Security and other retirement income, making jobs available to younger, unemployed workers who do not have other income potential.	Mandatory retirement can cause great economic hardship on older workers having financial obligations, as the average retirement income is less than half of working salary.
5. Mandatory retirement enables more opportunities for younger workers to advance and aids companies in recruitment, retrenchment, and replacement and allows infusion of new ideas.	The declining birthrate will mean proportionately fewer younger workers and the need for older workers. Additionally, mandatory retirement causes a loss of skills and experience, resulting in a reduced national output.

For Mandatory Retirement	Against Mandatory Retirement
6. It is more costly for employers to have an older worker on staff in terms of maintaining pension, health, and life insurance plans as well as salary levels.	Forced retirement causes an increased expense to government income-maintenance programs and pension programs. The declining birthrate will force a smaller labor force to support a larger retiree population.
7. Mandatory retirement provides opportunities and therefore aids in programs to promote women and minorities.	Studies have shown that the effect of legislation will be minimal. Additionally, women tend to enter the labor force later in life and need the extra years to gain pensions.

Figure 2. A Summary of Arguments for and Against Mandatory Retirement.

emotional deterioration and premature death. And older people, through various organizations, voiced their unwillingness to be cast on the "scrap heap of life" merely because of age. Comprising what may be our newest minority, older workers were demanding recognition of rights as a protected class—yet a class with political influence and growing numbers in relation to total population.

WHY NOW?

With strong opposition and a lack of substantive detail on the law's future effects, why did the bill pass so quickly and overwhelmingly? The reasons may be many, but as one spokesman observed, "Age discrimination is the last frontier of civil rights. . . . It's a very emotional issue, next to

motherhood. It's hard to vote against it!" There was sufficient logic to the argument that individual abilities to perform a job vary greatly and that age alone is an unfair determinant. And the climate was right in Washington, with
President Carter talking about human rights and the "Gray
Panthers" talking about the upcoming election year.

The timing of the bill, however, was also due to economic
factors. The growing financial burden of the Social Security
System impelled a search for solutions. By allowing some individuals to continue working, the payouts of the system
might be lessened. It may also be observed that at the time
of passage unemployment was regarded as relatively low. In
a period of extremely high unemployment, such a law would
be difficult to pass, because it would be seen as aggravating
unemployment by keeping older people in the work force,
holding scarce jobs.

Overall, however, it appears that the law passed because
it was seen as inevitable. As Representative Pepper stated,
"At long last, we will have eliminated ageism as we have
previously eliminated sexism and racism as a basis for discrimination in this country." Corporate executives widely
agreed that the drive toward flexible retirement was strong
and unrelenting. Indeed, it continues to be so. When asked
to give views on the legislation, many said they regarded it
as inevitable and believed that corporations must accept the
facts of social change and attune employment policies to individual merit rather than chronological age. As difficult as
this task may seem, these executives also saw potential benefits—reduced retirement benefit costs, improved ability to retain needed skills and experience, and improved employment stability in their organizations.

Retirement has been redefined. It is no longer an automatic
shift in gears from work to nonwork at a set age. It is, rather,
a voluntary withdrawal from the work force at the age that
best suits an individual's abilities, interests, and career plans.

CHAPTER TWO

MORE OLDER WORKERS, FEWER JOBS?

The response to the challenge of unemployment by many organizations has been simply to eliminate a segment of people—of certain age and older—from the labor force and put them into the retired category—Harold Sheppard, *The Graying of Working America*, p. 5.

Demographic factors have had a lot to do with federal legislation changing mandatory retirement. They also have a lot to do with our economy's need for talent, on the one hand, and the burden of supporting dependent people (whether young or old), on the other. Together with changes in the makeup of our population and our work force are such factors as the energy crisis, inflation, and recession. This chapter addresses these important considerations as a backdrop for examining the specifics of the legislation and its impact on management practices.

DEMOGRAPHIC CHANGES

The age characteristics of our population are changing and will continue to change into the next century. Simply put, the proportion of older people (aged 65 and over) in the population is increasing. Since 1900 this segment of the population has grown at a rate three times greater than that of the overall population.

This dramatic increase has been caused by a combination of social and medical factors. The birthrate in the United States steadily declined between 1880 and 1930, remained fairly steady in the 1930s, and began to rise in the 1940s, continuing until 1957. With the exception of 1970, the birthrate has dropped since then. At the same time, life expectancy has increased. In 1900, for example, life expectancy at birth was approximately 47 years. In 1970 it had increased to 71 years. Today a male 65 years old can expect to live 13.2 years longer, whereas a female at that age can expect to live 17.5 more years. The death rates for various age groups between age 15 and 64 have dropped steadily, by as much as one-half to three-fourths.

The net effect of these factors is that the percentage of the population who are 65 and over has increased dramatically. In 1900 those 65 and over accounted for 4% of the population; in 1930 the percentage was 5.4%; in 1950, 8.1%, and 1970, 9.9%. The trend is expected to continue into the twenty-first century. Projections indicate that by the year 2050 there will be more than 51 million persons over the age of 65 (compared with half that number today), or 16% of the total United States population (See Table 1).

At the same time that the proportion of older persons in the population has been increasing, participation in the labor force by older people has been decreasing. In 1950 almost 45% of males over the age of 65 were still working. By 1975 only 14% of all individuals age 65 and older remained in the work force.

EARLY RETIREMENT TRENDS

Several factors account for the trend toward earlier retirement. Clearly, employer-initiated early retirements have

Table 1.   Demographic Projections

Age Group	Numbers in Millions (%)				
	1975	1990	2000	2025	2050
Under 20	74.6 (35)	74.9 (31)	79.2 (30)	83.2 (28)	87.5 (27)
20–64	116.6 (55)	141.3 (58)	152.6 (58)	168.4 (56)	179.7 (57)
65+	22.3 (10)	28.9 (12)	30.6 (12)	48.1 (16)	51.2 (16)

Source: U.S. Bureau of the Census. *Current Population Reports,* Series P-25, No. 601. October, 1975. Tables 8, 11.

been a great impetus. A 1975 *Wall Street Journal* article noted that "to tighten operations, firms force men in 50's and 60's to retire early." The article stated that "mainly because of the sluggish economy, early retirement is no longer just an employee fringe benefit. It has become a useful, but controversial management tool. . . . The U.S. government may well be the biggest user of all." Many companies have adopted special programs designed to induce employees to retire early, so as to reduce staffing levels without disruptive layoffs or terminations, to "increase the effectiveness of management," and to reward long employee service. A major thrust seems to have been to create promotional opportunities within organizations by opening up positions blocked by older employees.

The beneficial organizational effects of early retirement are greater at management levels. Hence companies have focused on programs for salaried and executive-level employee groups. "Every time a chief executive leaves his position, 8 to 10 percent of managers below receive changes in assignments as well as salary adjustments," Eugene Jennings, a researcher on employee mobility, points out. In one corporation of 250,000 employees and 15,000 managers, the retirement of the chief executive alone meant reassignments for more than 1700 employees.

Of course, unions have pushed for earlier retirement, to open up opportunities for union member employment and union growth. The auto workers have long had provisions for "30 and out," providing generous retirement benefits after 30 years of service, regardless of age. The rubber workers union hailed a "25 years and out" pension provision as a "major breakthrough" in the industry, because the standard for the industry had been 30 years of service and the age of 55.

Particularly at managerial and salaried levels, many early retirements were disguised terminations. Exactly what proportion of "voluntary" early retirements are to some extent "forced" is not known. When given the option of retiring or being fired, older employees are prone to opt for the more socially favored retirement alternative. Forced or coerced, early retirements appear to be more common during recessionary periods, when companies are aiming to reduce staffing levels. Sheppard reported in *The Graying of Working America* that during the period 1969 to 1974, when joblessness rose from 3.5 to 5.6%, the percentage of people aged 60 to 64 who were not working increased four points. From 1973 to 1975 the percentage jumped five points.

When unemployment is relatively lower and the economy is growing, older workers are more readily able to obtain or retain employment. This is perhaps one reason the 1978 legislation was passed. The economy was enjoying a period of relative prosperity; unemployed younger workers did not represent a loud voice heard in Congress.

DEPENDENCY RATIO

Early retirement has its negative side for our economy, however. Even though mandatory retirement was introduced because of social needs as well as attitudes toward aging, its effects are clearly economic. The increasing life expectancy and the increased number of retirees have reversed the economic burden in our society, and the trend toward earlier retirement increases the burden even more. As historian Fischer described in *Growing Old in America*, "In early America, youth was kept in a condition of prolonged economic dependency upon age; in the nineteenth and early twentieth centuries, age often became economically dependent on youth. Prevailing attitudes toward age and youth were anchored in those material realities without being caused by them. If age and youth are to coexist, then neither youth nor age must be economically dependent upon each other" (Fischer, 1977 pp. 198–199).

The dependency ratio is simply the number of nonworkers per worker. If one calculates the ratio as the proportion of older people (age 65 and over) plus dependent younger people (under age 20) relative to the working population aged 20 to 64, the figure is approximately .8 or 1.25 workers for each dependent. With the declining numbers of young people in the population, relating to the declining birth rate, the ratio for the under-20 group to the 20 to 64 group is actually improving. However, with early retirement and growth of the over-65 age group, the dependency ratio is increasing (See Table 2). Additionally, the consideration of the 20 to

Table 2.   Dependency Ratios

Ratio	1975	1990	2000	2025	2050
Under 20:					
20–64	.64	.53	.52	.50	.49
65+:					
20–64	.19	.20	.20	.29	.28

Source: U.S. Bureau of the Census, *Current Population Reports*, Series P-25, No. 601, October 1975, Table 11.

64 age group as the labor force ignores the increased number of younger individuals currently attending university through ages 22 or more and entering the labor force after the age of 20.

THE CONCERNS

The rising dependency ratio is one concern of economists and officials responsible for Social Security benefits planning. Simply, each worker in the future will be supporting more nonworking older people. And this concern is a factor giving impetus to legislation allowing people to continue working rather than retiring. From a simple political point of view, the employed population may become less willing to pay higher taxes to support the elderly than they have been to pay taxes for the education of their own children.

Juanita Kreps, Secretary of Commerce, has even proposed that the minimum age for full eligibility for Social Security benefits be raised to age 68: "Perhaps the most clear-cut question posed by this demographic change is an economic one: How will the nation bear the cost of caring for so many old people? In a sense, the number of people each productive worker has to support won't have changed much, since the number of children is destined to shrink as the aged population grows. But the old are considerably more expensive to maintain" (*Newsweek*, "The Graying of America," p. 53).

Because of the greater burden imposed by older dependents than younger ones, another way to look at this concern is by examining retirement income. Social Security figures indicate that the ratio of wage earners to benefit recipients was 35 to 1 in 1945. In 1977 it was 3.2 to 1. Projections indicate that the ratio will be below 2 to 1 by the year 2035. Such decreases have strained the Social Security system. In the past 10 years the maximum tax has increased 233%. Trends suggest that Social Security taxes will have to rise to 25% of average income in a few years unless some changes are made (Harvey D. Shapiro, "Do Not Go Gently," *New York Times Magazine,* p. 41).

Changes in dependency ratios affect private and public pension plans as well. One example is the General Motors Corporation situation. In 1967 there were 10 workers for each retiree drawing a pension. Today that ratio is just 4 to 1, and predictions are that by the early 1990s, the ratio may be close to 1 to 1. "In other words, relatively fewer workers will be available to generate the revenues needed to support themselves, pay for other corporate needs and fund growing pension liabilities" (*Dun's Review,* "'Gray Rights' Retirement Fight," p. 84).

More serious problems, perhaps, exist in the Federal Civil Service Retirement System, the Uniformed Services Retirement System, and the more than 2000 state and local systems established for public employees. Recent studies have warned of the danger to the stability of public employee systems because of insufficient funding and overgenerous provisions.

Further, with a declining proportion of younger workers, our economy may very well need the talents of the older group as a vital labor pool. If the economy continues to grow as it has throughout our history, we will need to encourage older workers to stay in the work force as long as they are able. Some projections regarding the effects of future energy shortages suggest that we will rely more extensively on human labor as a substitute for costly and scarce energy. Should this be true, older workers will constitute a valuable resource, one we can ill-afford to retire.

THE EFFECTS OF INFLATION

Another important factor influencing retirement age policy is inflation. Retirees suffer from deteriorating purchasing power of fixed retirement incomes. As a result, many wish to return to work to supplement income. Employees eligible for early retirement often prefer to defer retirement to avoid the ravages of inflation, at least temporarily, and to maximize the basis of pension calculations. Certainly, early retirements look less attractive to prospective retirees when inflation is great. Benefits under private pensions are typically based on a calculation related to final pay. However liberal the early retirement discount, the benefit is based on a pay level that may be considerably below final pay at normal retirement age. Even if after-retirement cost-of-living adjustments are provided, they are calculated on a base that may be considered inadequate.

Furthermore, individuals who plan to obtain postretirement employment (usually another job in the same field) or start a second career (a different occupational pursuit) are now finding their opportunities limited. Those who expect to rely on earnings after retirement are cautious—new and attractive opportunities may not materialize. Hence they often wish to stay as long as they can on their present job.

Those individuals who do retire early tend to be those who have planned ahead to establish an adequate financial position. They have saved and invested in a manner that supplements benefits provided by pensions and by Social Security.

Those individuals who do return to new jobs or new careers frequently find that the pay is low. Companies have long practiced age discrimination in pay practices, compensating part-time or retirement jobs less than comparable jobs held by younger, full-time employees. Of course, the 1978 amendments extend protection against such discrimination to the age of 70, thus impelling companies to improve the pay for postretirement work.

"Double dipping" represents full-time employment of individuals who are also receiving full retirement income benefits. Common for military retirees, who leave the service with full benefits after 20 years of service, double dipping is becoming frequent among early retirees from private corporations. Because double dippers have the income cushion of retirement benefits, they are able to accept somewhat lower pay for jobs that are attractive to them. Many, however, receive as much or more for their services as they did in their preretirement careers.

SUMMARY

Changes in our population composition and changing economic conditions have created pressures for new retirement age policies. Often the forces are opposing and contradictory, such as the trend toward earlier retirement and the fear of the effects of inflation on retirement income. Yet the overall effect is to a mandate for increased consideration of the needs and problems of older people. The overwhelming support given the 1978 Age Discrimination Act amendments reflects this mandate.

CHAPTER THREE

NEW RULES GOVERNING RETIREMENT

It shall be unlawful for an employer (1) to fail or refuse to hire or to discharge any individual or otherwise discriminate against any individual with respect to his compensation, terms, conditions, or privileges of employment because of such individual's age—Age Discrimination in Employment Act.

With the 1978 Amendments to the Age Discrimination in Employment Act, mandatory retirement prior to the age of 70 is prohibited in companies employing 20 or more persons. In federal employment, age-based retirement restrictions are eliminated entirely. And by 1982 we may expect further federal and state legislation, eliminating the upper age limit for protection against age discrimination in companies as well.

For most workers the new law is effective January 1, 1979. But for employees subject to collectively bargained pension plans requiring retirement at 65, the law's effective date for superseding these labor agreements is the expiration of the agreements or January 1, 1980, whichever comes first.

NEW FEDERAL AGE AMENDMENTS SIGNED

At the White House Rose Garden ceremony, where President Carter signed the bill April 6, 1978, the President said, "This bill provides fairness and equity in protecting older workers from discrimination in employment." The measure, for which momentum had been building in Congress for several years, has the effect of permitting (but not requiring) another 5 years of employment for millions of individuals who would otherwise be forced to retire at age 65.

However, several employee groups are exempted from the amendments, in addition to employers with fewer than 20 employees. First, the upper age limit will not become effective for tenured college and university professors until July 1, 1982. University administrators had argued that because of static employment levels, forced retirements were necessary to provide opportunities for the hiring and promotion of younger professors, particularly women and minorities.

The second exemption is for corporate executives and other high-level policy makers. These persons may still be forced to retire at the age of 65 if they are entitled to employer-financed retirement benefits totaling at least $27,000 annually. The amount must be nonforfeitable and must not include employee contributions. It does not include Social Security. A pension is defined as a benefit paid from pension plans, savings, deferred earnings, or a combination of these plans.

The law was clearly intended to be a matter of employment policy and thus promotion of employment opportunities for older workers. It was not intended to ensure full equality of treatment of employees. Accordingly, required changes in benefit and pension plan provisions are not spelled out in the law and are yet to be determined through regulations and court interpretations (see Chapter 6). It appears that under the 1978 amendments, employers are not required to provide additional benefits to employees who remain beyond the normal retirement date. Thus employers may stop contributing to an employee pension plan after the "normal" retirement age, and employees who elect to work beyond this age will typically forego their retirement benefits until they actually do retire. Years of service beyond the age of 65 need not be credited to an employee for purposes of determining pension benefits on retirement. Similarly, the law apparently does not require employers to provide equal benefits (or contributions/costs) to employees over the age of 65 that are provided to employees under the age of 65. This is considered important to employers, because medical costs and life insurance costs rise dramatically after that age.

It is likely, however, that differentials in employee benefits will not be tolerated very long, because they fly in the face of the human rights and equal employment opportunity values that gave rise to the legislation. Differential treatment of employees over 65 is clearly a void in the coverage of the Age Discrimination in Employment Act (ADEA) which will be filled with future legislation.

In fact, the age-70 limit is certainly a temporary constraint. After the 1978 amendments were enacted, Claude Pepper promptly submitted new proposed legislation eliminating any retirement age. Elimination of age as a factor in employment has always been and will continue to be the aim of the proponents.

NEW STATE LAWS

While Congress deliberated the merits of ending mandatory retirement, various state legislatures also considered legislation. At one count 26 states were considering various laws modifying mandatory retirement. California, Connecticut, Florida, Maine, and Minnesota have passed laws affecting mandatory retirement of employees in the private sector. Legislative proposals have been considered in New Jersey, Pennsylvania, Colorado, Illinois, Massachusetts, Minnesota, New York, and Washington.

Effective January 1, 1978, mandatory retirement is banned in California at any age for any employer of over five workers. The effective date is January 1, 1980 if a collective bargaining agreement or pension plan in effect December 31, 1977 had imposed mandatory retirement. If a collective bargaining contract expires prior to the 1980 date, the law's prohibition of mandatory retirement goes into effect at that time.

The California law is, to many observers, a model of brevity, if not clarity. It reads as follows:

> The Legislature of the State of California finds and declares that the use of chronological age as an indicator of ability to perform on the job and the practice of mandatory retirement from employment are obsolete and cruel practices. The downward trend toward involuntary retirement at ages from 55 years represents a highly undesirable development in the utilization of California's worker resources. In addition, this practice is now imposing serious stresses on our economy and in particular on pension systems and other income maintenance systems.
>
> . . . It is an unlawful employment practice for an employer to refuse to hire or employ, or to discharge, dismiss, reduce, suspend, or demote, any individual over the age of 40 on the ground of age, except in cases where the law compels or provides for such action. This section shall not be construed to make unlawful the rejection or termination of employment where the individual applicant or employee failed to meet bona fide requirements for the job or position sought or held, or to require any changes in any bona fide retirement or pen-

sion programs or existing collective bargaining agreements during the life of the contract, or for two years after the effective date of this section, whichever comes first, nor shall this section preclude such physical or medical examinations of applicants and employees as an employer may make or have made to determine fitness for the job or position sought or held.

Promotions within the existing staff, hiring or promotion on the basis of experience and training, rehiring on the basis of seniority and prior service with the employer, or hiring under an established recruiting program . . . shall not, in and of themselves, constitute a violation of this section.

Technically, the law does not ban mandatory retirement policies of employers. Rather, it provides that:

Every employer in this state, except a public agency, shall permit any employee who indicates in writing a desire in a reasonable time and can demonstrate the ability to do so, to continue his employment beyond the normal retirement date contained in any private pension or retirement plan. Such employment shall continue so long as the employee demonstrates his ability to perform the functions of the job adequately and the employer is satisfied with the quality of work performed.

Further, the law states that employers are not required to change funding, benefit levels, or formulas of any existing retirement plan. Thus accruals do not appear to be required for employee service after the normal retirement date. However, by inference, pension and insurance plans established after January 1, 1978 may be required to provide for post-normal retirement date accruals and continuation of insurance coverage on a prenormal retirement date basis. This apparent requirement is not detailed in the law.

The California law is significant because it goes beyond the federal age discrimination law. That there is no upper age limit, that future retirement benefits may be modified, and demonstration of adequate job performance by an individual are all features of the California law not found in the federal law. It is possible that ERISA (The Federal Employee Retirement Income Security Act) preempts such state laws dealing with benefit plan design. However, the federal ADEA and the new amendments do not preempt state law if the state law is more liberal. California protects all employees over the age of 40; thus the federal age limit of 70 is academic in this state.

A company operating in California and other states will likely face varying standards for mandatory retirement practices and may be forced as a practical matter to abandon mandatory retirement as a corporate policy. Following California's action has come similar action in Maine, Connecticut, and Minnesota. The Maine statute requires that mandatory retirement be eliminated in the private sector by 1980. Effective January 1979, most Connecticut corporate employees cannot be required to retire at any age. State and municipal employees and teachers, however, can still be forced to retire at the age of 70. The law does not apply to the retirement of employees, at any age, who receive annual retirement benefits of $27,000 exclusive of Social Security benefits. Unlike the ADEA exemption, however, benefits attributable to employee contributions may be counted for this purpose. Unlike California and Minnesota, Connecticut does not require employees to inform employers of their intent to remain beyond the normal retirement date. Instead, employees are only required to inform their employers at least 30 days prior to their actual retirement date.

The Minnesota law raises the earliest permissible mandatory retirement age for most employees to the age of 70. It differs from the federal law in that it covers companies with fewer than 20 employees, effective June 1, 1980. Also, it is possible that the law will be interpreted as requiring retirement plan accruals beyond the employee's normal retirement date. The Minnesota law permits retirement at 65 of a "professional, executive or administrative employee" and calculates the $27,000 income test somewhat differently than under federal law. In most aspects, then, this state law adds little to the rights already guaranteed to employees covered by federal law.

BACKGROUND OF THE AGE DISCRIMINATION LAW

ADEA was the first federal law prohibiting discrimination based on age. Enacted in 1967, the act protected persons aged 40 through 64 for the purpose of promoting employment of older persons based on their ability rather than their age. The act also sought to prohibit arbitrary age discrimination in employment, to help employers and workers find ways of meeting problems arising from the impact of age on employment.

It was not the first age discrimination law in the United States, however. Prior to the ADEA's enactment, 21 states had passed laws relating to age discrimination. Many state laws are similar to the ADEA. By 1976, 42 states and the District of Columbia had passed such laws. Thirteen of these states (Alaska, Connecticut, Florida, Hawaii, Illinois, Iowa, Maine, Maryland, Montana, Nevada, New Jersey, New Mexico, and South Carolina) have no statutory upper age limits for protection; rather, they concentrate on hiring, terms, conditions, or privileges of employment. None specifically bans mandatory retirement. Five of the states (Colorado, Michigan, New York, Oregon, and South Dakota) and the District of Columbia protect workers against age discrimination from the age of 18.

In 1974 the ADEA was amended to include public employees at federal, state, and local levels, who were not previously covered by the act. Under this amendment protection was extended to the age of 70 for federal employees.

How were the age limits selected under the ADEA? The sponsors of the original age discrimination act noted that 40 "is the age where, according to information currently available, age discrimination generally seems to start. Age 65 is the age at which social security benefits become available."

AGE DISCRIMINATION
LITIGATION

Since 1967 an estimated $28 million has been paid in settlements to approximately 8000 individuals adversely affected by age discrimination. Most of these payments have included back pay from the date of violation together with accrued benefits that would have been earned or given. In a few cases the courts have granted compensatory damages for "pain and suffering and liquidated damages under the ADEA." In one case (Rogers v. Exxon Research and Engineering Co.) the court ruled in favor of the claimant, a chemist forced to retire at age 60. Damages were awarded for "adverse impact on his physical and emotional wellbeing which had been conclusively shown to have been the proximate result of the defendant's illegal discrimination" (Schlei and Grossman, 1976).

The Employment Standards Administration of the Department of Labor initially had responsibility for enforcing the ADEA. Beginning July 1979, however, responsibility will rest with the Equal Employment Opportunity Commission under an executive order to consolidate enforcement activities. In 1977 the Department of Labor reported that the number of complaints, court cases, violations, and subsequently due damages have increased significantly each year since 1968. "The large increases in the number of complaints received during the past three years may be attributable to a greater awareness of the provisions of the ADEA on the part of employees, job applicants and retirees, accompanied by a willingness to contest alleged illegal employment practices." In 1976, there were 8313 compliance actions undertaken, and violations amounted to $8.3 million. "Illegal discharges" (forced retirements) accounted for over 20% of the cases heard, a 41% increase over 1975.

In 1973 Standard Oil of California signed a consent decree to reinstate 120 employees who were forced to retire early. Back pay to these employees exceeded $2 million. Other cases have included Pan American World Airways (400 employees), Sandia Corporation (230 employees), Chessie System (300), Liggett and Myers (125), and American Motors (63). With the increase in age protection to 70 and the significantly greater awareness of age discrimination law resulting from the passage of the 1978 amendments, the number of cases is likely to increase dramatically in the years ahead.

EXCEPTIONS TO THE LAW

Every rule seems to have its exception, especially when it is the product of the legislative process. Section 4(f) of the ADEA originally contained three general exceptions to the provisions. These exceptions have been subjected to litigation and to amendment. Each has an effect on mandatory retirement. Hence a brief discussion of them is appropriate. The exceptions are: (1) where age is a bona fide occupational qualification, (2) to observe the terms of a bona fide seniority system or employee benefit plan, and (3) to discharge or otherwise discipline an individual for good cause. The second of these [Section 4(f)(2)] was widely used as the basis for supporting mandatory retirement provisions in court cases. The most famous of these cases, the only one to reach the Supreme Court, was United Air Lines v. McMann. The appeals court held that a pre-65 mandatory retirement age under a pension plan, even one established prior to 1967, was a "subterfuge to evade the Act's purpose of prohibiting arbitrary age discrimination." "Stated otherwise, there must be some reason other than age for a plan, or a provision of a plan, which discriminates between employees of different ages." However, the Supreme Court reversed this ruling, stating that the exception provided in section 4(f)(2) should be read to permit mandatory retirement.

These cases are now moot with the 1978 amendments. Retirements may not be forced, regardless of pension plan provisions, prior to age of 70. Attention focused on the McMann case and widespread dissatisfaction with the ultimate decision were likely factors contributing to support for the 1978 legislation removing the exception.

Exceptions (1) and (3) remain in effect, and court cases provide perspective of their interpretation and practical application by employers. The burden of proof in establishing the applicability of an exception rests with the employer, not with the plaintiff or the government. Each of these two exceptions is discussed briefly below.

BFOQS

Section 4(f)(1) reads as follows:

> It shall not be unlawful for an employer, employment agency or labor organization to take any action otherwise prohibited . . . where age is a bona fide occupational qualification reasonably necessary to the normal operation of the particular business, or where the differentiation is based on reasonable factors other than age.

Bona fide occupational qualifications (BFOQs) have been in the limelight of personnel management since the passage of Title VII of the Civil Rights Act. Employers have been impelled by equal employment law and court cases to define job requirements in a manner free of race and sex bias. Under the ADEA they are impelled to remove age bias as well.

But the BFOQ exception in the ADEA has resulted in conflicting interpretations by different courts of appeals. In two similar decisions concerning bus drivers (Hogdson v. Greyhound Lines, Inc. and Usery v. Tamiami Trail Tours, Inc.) a maximum age limit for the hiring of bus drivers was challenged. In one case the age was 40; in the other the age was 35. Based primarily on safety statistics of older drivers, the court reversed a district ruling in the Hodgson case and sustained Greyhound's hiring policy. Review of the case was refused by the Supreme Court. However, a contrary decision was reached in a case involving forced retirement of a test pilot from McDonnell-Douglas Corporation (Houghton v. McDonnell-Douglas Corporation). In reversing a district court decision, the Eighth Circuit Court of Appeals ruled that the age of a test pilot who was over 50 years old was not a bona fide occupational qualification justifying downgrading to a nonflying position. The court stated, "there was no evidence that a test pilot's ability to perform his duties, both safely and effectively, was impaired in such a manner as to justify the imposition of the arbitrary age limit applied by the Company."

The ADEA also provides that the law is not violated if the "differentiation is based on reasonable factors other than age." Several factors supporting such a reasonable differentiation have been identified by the Department of Labor:

- Physical fitness requirements, so long as the minimum standards are reasonably necessary . . . and are uniformly applied.

- Evaluation factors as quantity or quality of production.

- Conditions as to the number or schedule of hours to be worked.

Of course, determination of what is reasonable rests on a case-by-case evaluation. However, one parameter has been defined: "The general assertion that the average cost of employing older workers is higher than the average cost of employing younger workers as a group will not be recognized . . . as a valid differentiation" (Schlei and Grossman, 1976).

It is pertinent to note that in some cases age-based employment requirements (mandatory retirement age) have been challenged under the equal protection clause of the Constitution (a basis not applicable to private employers). One case involved forced retirement of a uniformed state police officer in Massachusetts at the age of 50. The officer, Robert Murgia, demonstrated he was physically fit and otherwise able to perform all duties required. Yet state policy mandated his retirement at 50. In the final decision on his case, the U.S. Supreme Court ruled that the policy was rationally based, as "the objective of assuring physical fitness is rationally furthered by a maximum age limitation." The state merely selected a method of determining physical fitness that is not the "best means of achieving this purpose." In sum, mandatory retirement at *some* age is rational in a physically demanding job, and therefore legal under the fourteenth amendment. Although 50 may not be the age and other forms of competency tests could be applied, the constitution is not violated by the application of an age limit.

Finally, it should be noted that the best way to avoid allegations of discrimination under job requirements that are not bona fide is to eliminate age as a job requirement. That may not be as difficult as it seems, as age is usually a convenient summary of multiple factors relating to physical condition, abilities, and skills. AT&T, as one employer, has declared in a personnel policy statement that not any of its jobs requires a certain age. Age is not a BFOQ in the Bell System.

DISCHARGE FOR GOOD CAUSE

Section 4(f)(3) reads as follows: "It shall not be unlawful for an employer, employment agency or labor organization to discharge or otherwise discipline an individual for good cause." "Good causes" for discharge are similar to the factors listed as being support for "reasonable differentiation" noted above. Court decisions in recent discharge cases under ADEA indicate to employers that accurate and substantial evidence of individual performance and competence is necessary as a basis for personnel actions that adversely affect protected employees.

In the recent case of Mistretta v. Sandia Corporation (1977) the theme of Sandia's defense was that performance appraisals were the main ingredients in layoff decisions that adversely affected a number of older employees in 1973. In the court's decision, District Court Judge Mechem concluded:

> The system is extremely subjective and has never been validated. Supervisors were not told to consider specific criteria in their ratings . . . the evaluations were based on best judgment and opinion of the evaluators, but were not based on any definite identifiable criteria based on quality or quantity of work or specific performances that were supported by some kind of record. Courts have condemned subjective standards as fostering discrimination.

Other age discrimination decisions which have pointed to the need for valid performance appraisals include Brito v. Zia Co., 478 F. 2d 1200, Muller v. U.S. Steel, 509 F. 2d 923 (10th Cir. 1975), Rich v. Martin-Marietta, 522 F. 2d at 350, and Sarcini v. Missouri Pacific Railway Company, 431 F. Supp. 389, 393 (1977).

Judge Mechem noted several problems with the system used by Sandia, which was derived from Bell System policy (Sandia is a subsidiary of Western Electric Company). He observed:

> . . . subjective systems are often corrupted by personal bias. . . . When a decision involves an individual in the protected age group, the decision must be based on abilities rather than age. Management's concern about the increasing age of its staff, reduced hiring, new technical developments, an emphasis on recruiting and advancing young Ph.D.s might not violate ADEA in themselves, but these policies and attitudes could easily be reflected in subjective performance ratings.

In ruling against Sandia he concluded:

> The evidence presented (by Sandia) is not sufficient to prove or disprove the contention that at Sandia performance declines with age, but there is sufficient circumstantial evidence to indicate that age bias and age based policies appear throughout the performance rating process to the detriment of the protected age group.

Chapters 7, 8, and 9 of this book examine the implications of these cases for management practice. Suggestions are offered for development of evaluation procedures and techniques that will minimize the risk of age bias.

CONCLUSION

The ADEA and relevant state laws set the stage for elimination of employment discrimination based on age. The 1978 amendments to the ADEA expand ages of the protected group of employees from 40 through 64 to 40 through 69. Further, the law closes a major exemption represented by section 4(f)(2), which allowed involuntary retirements under provisions of an established pension or retirement benefit plan.

In dissenting from the opinion of the Supreme Court in the United Airlines v. McMann case, Justice Thurgood Marshall observed that the legal stage being set was actually intended with the passage of the ADEA in 1967. The courts, in his view, have misinterpreted the letter and intent of the ADEA with regards to section 4(f)(2). He wrote:

The mischief the Court fashions today may be short lived. Both the House and Senate have passed amendments to the Act. The amendments expressly provide that the involuntary retirement of employees shall not be permitted or required pursuant to any employee benefit plan. Thus today's decision may have virtually no prospective effect. But the Committee reports of both Houses make plain that, properly understood, the existing Act already prohibits involuntary retirement, and that the Amendment is only a clarification necessitated by court decisions misconstruing congressional intent. . . . the Court today has also misconstrued congressional intent and has thereby deprived many older workers of the protection which Congress sought to afford.

PART TWO
MANAGEMENT STRATEGIES

CHAPTER FOUR

INTRODUCING MORE FLEXIBLE RETIREMENT

In recent years great interest has been shown in the possibility of creating more flexibility. . . . Several international organizations have conducted studies and scientists in many countries have written on the relations of work, age, and retirement. Doctors, psychologists, and sociologists have recognized that a sudden switch from working life to full retirement can be detrimental to many workers and have suggested that work arrangements be designed to enable workers to prepare themselves for full retirement—Kenneth Bratthall, "Flexible Retirement and the New Swedish Partial Pension Scheme," *Industrial Gerontology.*

Simply put, flexible retirement means that employees are allowed to select their own retirement date. More broadly, it means that they may consider alternatives to abrupt retirement, such as gradual retirement, modified work arrangements, or second careers. Just as employees make their own decisions regarding their vocations, job choices, relocations, and other career decisions, employees make their own retirement timing decisions. And with the lifting of mandatory retirement to the age of 70 for employer policies, most employees now face the responsibility of deciding for themselves when they should retire.

In a sense, many companies have had "flexible retirement" for some time. When interest developed in early retirement, many pension plans were modified to allow retirements prior to the normal or mandatory retirement age. Plans were amended to allow early retirements with reductions in retirement benefits calculated to account for the greater number of years during which benefits would be received ("actuarial reduction"). Then, to induce employees to retire early, many employers liberalized the benefits by removing or reducing the discount in benefits. For example, many employers allowed voluntary early retirement at the age of 62 or later without reduction in benefits, and before the age of 62 with a lower rate of discount in benefits. Additionally, some employers would provide a "make-up" supplemental payment for early retirees until the age of 62 to compensate for Social Security benefits. This meant that the employees were free to retire at any of a series of ages without reduction in benefits (other than the loss of possible salary increases on which final pay-based benefits might have been calculated).

Of course, the "30 years and out" provisions of the auto and rubber worker contracts also enable "flexible" retirement timing by eligible individuals. Once the years of service are accrued, it is up to the individual to determine what age is desired for retirement. Recent experience at General Motors indicates that eight out of nine auto workers opt to retire early when their requisite 30 years of service have accrued. One in fifty stays on to the age of 68, which has been General Motors mandatory retirement age.

Retirement timing appears to be determined by countervailing forces of two sets of variables. Individuals weigh the factors in deciding when they will retire. Factors that tend to push retirement age up (defer retirement timing) are fear of inflation, economic necessity of working, job satisfaction, fear of aging and death, and perceptions that retirement would not be satisfying. Factors that tend to accelerate retirement timing (early retirements) include adequacy of income and pension benefits, adequacy of Social Security benefits, poor health, job dissatisfaction, opportunity for a second career, decline in performance, threat of change (e.g., technological obsolescence), pressures from younger workers, and a generally positive view toward retirement. To be workable, then, flexible retirement policies must guide individuals to an understanding and evaluation of these factors so that they will opt for retirement at times best suited personally to their own and the company's needs. Chapter 12 considers further the manner by which employees decide when they will retire.

NEW MANAGEMENT TOOLS REQUIRED

Flexible retirement does not become reality merely by eliminating mandatory retirement. The problem of managing older employees who have different career interests and different levels of abilities is far more complex than simply setting a retirement age policy. Margaret Kuhn, leader of the Gray Panthers, observed in an article entitled, "After Mandatory Retirement, What?" that "Rather than seeing the end of mandatory retirement as the solution, we should consider a broad range of options that would make the structure of education, work, and leisure more flexible." She suggested that "A variety of options might include sabbatical leaves, part-time or shared work, and the facilitating of mid-career changes. Retirement could be optional and flexible. We could encourage those who desire to use some of their Social Security benefits to take a sabbatical leave in search of education, training, and re-evaluation of life directions possibly toward new careers."

Because the age-70 limit is likely to be a temporary age

limit, companies are advised to introduce policies and programs that will enable employees, at any age, to consider
their career options and make their own decisions regarding
their work and their personal development. Kuhn observed,
"In the long run, we anticipate that workers of various ages
will feel empowered by the choice to improve their work
style, the emergence of job fluidity, and the new consideration of leisure time. They will see the possibility of exercising
further control over the administration, organization and
structure of the workplace." Regardless of how much influence employees may want, it is certain that they *now* hold
all the cards regarding retirement timing before the age
of 70.

To introduce flexible retirement effectively, employers
need six basic kinds of tools. Each is discussed briefly in this
chapter:

1   Planning for orderly management succession.

2   Employee communications and counseling focused on the
needs and concerns of the older workers.

3   Gradual retirement options that allow reduction of the time
devoted to work.

4   Job modification options that allow changes in the content
of work performed.

5   Career renewal options that allow the individuals to change
their career emphasis and more fully develop their capabilities.

6   Termination procedures that allow the employer to face up
to inadequate performance of older workers and take legal personnel actions to "force them to retire" for good cause.

Of course, underlying these tools is the need for a flexible
retirement benefit system that allows older workers to consider different ages for retirement without major personal
financial penalty. It is also assumed that companies offering
flexible retirement already have other basic human resource

management systems and policies in place and working for all age groups (e.g., recruitment, training and development, appraisal, salary administration, internal placement, and job descriptions).

These tools (or retirement options) are considered basic human resource management techniques in a few companies and are being adopted for broad reasons of affirmative action programming in others. To many, however, they simply make good management sense as tools for getting the best performance from employees and maintaining a strong and viable work force. None is a blue-sky idea; each has been applied and tested and found to be workable as a practical management tool.

MANAGEMENT SUCCESSION PLANNING

With a mandatory retirement age, the attrition from management ranks is predictable on the basis of age. Many traditional manpower planning models based plans for succession on the predictable aging of cohort groups, with a group moving up a level as the older executives retire. However, with the advent of early retirement options and the raising of the mandatory retirement age to 70, the predictability related to age is somewhat lessened. With no upper limit for continued employment, chronological age is even less useful a determinant.

In management succession planning, then, an important consideration must be the assessment of the probability of retirement of managers holding key career positions. Some may be exempted from the 1978 ADEA amendments by virtue of their position and pension eligibility. Most, however, will have the option of retiring early, retiring at the normal retirement age, or retiring later on. A survey should be made to determine the timing preferences and retirement plans, if any, of the individuals holding such positions as early as the age of 50, so that an orderly succession may be planned and candidates directed to prepare for positions expected to be vacated.

Age cohort analysis is still a useful tool. Simply list all managers, by name and current position by 5-year age classifications. Then consider:

- Who are likely to retire early?

- Who are likely to stay?

- Who are the stronger performers, whom you would like to stay on longer?

A name-by-name assessment provides a useful overview of the potential talent losses and potential career position blockages.

With this information as a basis, a simple forecast of vacancies and managerial staffing requirements may be estimated. Obviously, the specific positions that must be filled are not precisely known, but the forecast provides a useful plan for guiding development and recruitment activities.

When executives who are not the best performers and lack potential for increased responsibility wish to stay on, positions may be modified and organizational relationships changed. Alternatively, management can face up to these individuals and evaluate current performance and future job prospects, thus inducing the individuals to opt for retirement as an alternative more desirable than embarrassment in the company. In many instances, however, blockages by poorly performing executives are few, and the individuals are not likely to stay on long when the trend among their cohorts is toward early retirement. Of course, if the individual executives qualify under the ADEA exemption, they may be forced to retire at the age of 65 or later.

EMPLOYEE COMMUNICATIONS
AND COUNSELING

Employees should be well informed regarding their rights and responsibilities regarding continued employment as they grow older. Many companies have published descriptions of the new age discrimination amendments and their effects on company programs. They have published various booklets, produced audiovisual presentations, and written personal letters to inform employees about retirement benefits programs and their rights under them. Granted, the requirements for explanation of benefits under ERISA have impelled much of this communications activity, but companies have frequently gone far beyond the legal requirements.

Some companies have provided self-analysis and career planning programs to employees to help them evaluate their personal abilities, limitations, interests, goals, and plans. Published materials are often provided, along with group workshops and frequent guest speakers. The career perspective helps downplay the "crisis" orientation of many pre-retirement communications.

Counseling and guidance by company staff or outside personnel has also helped older employees both to understand the decisions they must make and to prepare for the adjustment to retirement. Of course, counseling often helps individuals consider alternate career options as well as total retirement. Some companies have cooperated in sponsoring community counseling centers to aid individual career and retirement planning, as well as to help solve alcoholism, drug, and other life adjustment problems.

An immediate "knee jerk" reaction of many employers to the proposed 1978 legislation was to fear the worst of an end to mandatory retirement. Accordingly, communications to employees (if any) and comments in the mass media voiced management concerns about "eliminating deadwood," keeping promotional channels open through forced retirements, and the need for predictability of retirements for human resource planning. It is important, therefore, for employers to communicate in a positive manner to employees regarding company retirement policy changes and available retirement planning options and resources. Chapters 14, 15, and 16 discuss the steps that may be taken by companies for effective ways to help employees plan for retirement.

GRADUAL RETIREMENT

One way to reduce employee dependence on work and increase readiness for full-time retirement is "gradual retirement." In its various forms this technique involves a reduction of the amount of time an individual devotes to work and an increase in the amount of time devoted to leisure or retirement-oriented activities.

One form of gradual retirement is the reduced workweek. An employee eligible for retirement (full retirement benefits) may work a reduced number of hours per day or per week. Pay may or may not be reduced accordingly, depending on management policies. On professional and managerial jobs the pay would normally be kept whole. The amount of time worked may be gradually reduced, until full-time withdrawal from work is achieved.

Increasingly longer vacation periods may also reduce time spent in the work force for older workers and help them adjust to the idea of retirement. Vacation allowances may sharply increase after the age of 60, to six or eight weeks, for this purpose.

Leaves and sabbaticals, involving extended periods of time away from work, may also be useful. Spending a year assisting the United Way Campaign or on a government exchange program or teaching can both contribute to society and help ease the transition from work to retirement. Usually self-initiated leaves involve a reduced pay arrangement; social service leaves are frequently covered by company programs that do not reduce pay significantly.

In other instances, older workers may be offered part-time rather than full-time work. Sometimes whole jobs may be shared by two part-time workers. Such arrangements have proven workable for older persons returning to the work force (e.g., older women), and certainly this system is applicable as a form of gradual retirement. It is another way of handling a reduced work week.

Finally, many companies have offered postretirement employment to workers. Employees may be induced to retire voluntarily, say, at the age of 62, and then be offered the opportunity to continue working thereafter on a year-to-year contract basis. Under a flexible retirement policy, employees would be allowed to retire, try it out, and then return to work should they wish. Of course, employees have the right to apply for jobs without age as a consideration, but under this technique specific postretirement work opportunities would be held out to capable employees.

The technique has been used frequently in cases of specialists and managers whose services were felt to be needed. Often, consulting arrangements are established. In other instances, consulting arrangements are extended to ease the retirement of key managers. In many cases their consulting is not what is wanted, though—their departure is. It is advisable to employ individuals after retirement only for bona fide work, not as a subterfuge to induce retirement.

It should be emphasized that under the ADEA a retired employee may reapply for a job with protection against age discrimination. There is no excuse for failure to hire, reads the law. Any retiree aged 40 through 69 may reapply for the job previously held or any other job and receive consideration on equal terms with other applicants. Preferential consideration need not be given former employees, but neither may former employees be discouraged because of their status. Typically, the individual, if rehired, is required to assume active employee status and forego retiree status under the pension plan. Pension benefits are not readjusted; no additional service credits are given while the employee continues working. AT&T, for one, has carefully spelled out in its personnel policies the rules under which retirees may return to work. Of course, an employer cannot require an employee who retired from another company to forego benefits from that employer. "Double dipping" can be controlled only from the same trough.

CAREER RENEWAL

A third approach to flexible retirement involves redirecting the careers of older employees. As individuals approach retirement eligibility, they are often impelled to reconsider goals not yet achieved, reassess personal strengths and limitations, and launch a vigorous program of personal career development and achievement.

Career planning programs provide individual employees with resources for self-analysis and career development. Developed primarily for "younger, high-potential" employees, these programs help evaluate personal abilities, interests, experience, and future goals and plans. Career planning can include self-study materials, group workshops or seminars, and counseling by managers or staff. For older workers such materials and programs may be tailored to the particular issues and interests that are relevant to the decisions regarding retirement and career renewal. They are a broader form of simple preretirement counseling and retirement preparation programs commonly offered older employees (see Chapter 15).

Career planning programs aid management in planning and forecasting staffing requirements. Concurrently, they help individuals make their own retirement timing decisions. In the typical career planning program, employees voice their career development goals, job preferences, and personal development activities to management, as an input to human resource planning. Career renewal among older employees similarly represents plans to retire, continue for a time on the same job, or change jobs or career directions. Voicing these plans helps management plan and forecast staffing needs relating to otherwise uncertain retirement timing.

Under the California and Minnesota laws, for example, employees are required to inform their employers of their intention to work past the normal retirement date. There is no reason why companies in California and elsewhere can not establish a procedure for guiding individual career planning and for finding out what older employees' career plans are. A loudly voiced objection to the mandatory retirement legislation in Washington was the increased *uncertainty* of retirement timing created by lifting the age ceiling. Career planning can help minimize the risk of imbalanced staffing or unpredicted staffing requirements. All employees at, say, the age of 55 or within 5 years of full retirement eligibility may be asked their intentions and offered specific assistance in career planning to help think the matter through.

To help ease the transition to retirement or to second careers, some companies have broadened their educational assistance program to aid employees. IBM, for example, allows employees as early as 52 to receive $500 per year to cover costs of courses taken in accredited institutions. The program begins 3 years before retirement and continues for 2 years after retirement.

Other companies have expanded their in-house training and development resources to help equip employees for career changes. Retraining of older workers for jobs that may better suit their personal interests and abilities is considered a logical alternative to forced retirements.

The Rego Company, a subsidiary of the Marmon Group, has a formal program for easing the transition to retirement. One year prior to retirement, employees receive time off for personal business planning and paid physical examinations. After 3 months they receive financial counseling with persons in the personnel department. In these discussions the employees help define criteria for selection of their replacements. The last 6 months are spent training the replacement, and the employee is given increasing amounts of personal time off.

As another example, the State of Florida will transfer state employees over the age of 65 to part-time work if they desire. They are paid accordingly, but with no reduction in pension benefits when they do retire. Sweden passed a new national "partial-pension scheme" in 1976 which allows workers between the ages of 60 and 65 to reduce their working hours and draw partial pensions accordingly as preparation for full retirement. In Sweden, pension benefits under this system accrue until the age of 70.

MODIFIED JOB REQUIREMENTS

Many older employees wish to continue working beyond 65 but do not wish to change careers or reduce the time devoted to their work. They simply wish to stay on their jobs or to take on jobs that are similar to work they have been doing during their careers. A maximum of job continuity and a minimum of disruptive change are the primary aims of modifying the jobs performed by older employees.

To accommodate the interests of older workers and at the same time to meet company needs in human resource planning, the *content* of work performed may be modified. The aim is to match the work with the abilities and interests of older workers in a manner that also furthers the purpose of management. Simply put, some older employees who wish to defer retirement may wish changes in the work they are doing, and these changes may very well be compatible with company needs.

Three basic kinds of job changes are considered here: reduction of job scope, downgrading of position, and special assignments. Each allows employees to use the particular skills and abilities accrued and applied during their careers without major career redirection or gradual withdrawal from work.

Reducing the scope of a job performed involves modifying the responsibilities, demands, and related conditions of a job. For example, a sales representative may have traveled a large area for a number of years. The number of customers has increased, and many of the customers are younger and more demanding. Also, the travail of traveling long distances may be considered a bit undesirable. Yet the sales representative would prefer to stay on the job rather than retire, if only the job could be adapted somewhat. Accordingly, the company split the sales territory, assigning another sales representative to assume the responsibility for about half the accounts. The senior employee would help the new representative get to know the customers, but not as a supervisor. The net result was that the older employee felt relieved to have a reduced travel and work burden and yet pleased to be able to continue on the job. In this instance the company continued the pay at the previous level, on an exception ("red circle") basis, although a reduced pay level would have been justified.

As Soloman Barkin, a labor economist, has observed:

Job redesign is a means of retaining the services of older workers of proved efficiency, but for whom conditions of work are unfavorable. . . . Job redesign may therefore exercise a far more profound effect on the retention of jobs than has been realized. Its influence is subtle. Even so, the effects are important. Older people who stay in their jobs may continue to offer all the fruits of their developed skill, but in moving to other jobs, they may be slower to adjust, their relative contribution may be less and such transfers add to training costs both in the job vacated and the job being entered (Barkin, 1970).

Operative jobs may be simplified to eliminate physical hazards or tasks that may have become unduly taxing to an individual. Professional and technical jobs may be restructured to take advantage of individual strengths and minimize demands that are difficult because of declining competencies. Rarely does an individual fall significantly short of the demands of a position; usually, only minor job modifications are necessary. It is particularly easy to modify the content of managerial positions so as to better utilize the talents of incumbents by reallocating functions and organizational responsibilities.

There are also many instances where a downgrading of assignment is a suitable way of modifying work demands for older employees who wish to continue in their specialty. Supervisors often become weary of the demands of management responsibilities and welcome a change to "go back to the bench." Company officers step back to plant or regional manager positions to allow others to assume the broader responsibilities. Often downgrading of assignments occurs in companies as a result of organizational restructuring. Here the intent is to serve company needs, but the effect is often a welcome modification of individual work demands.

Granted, there has long been social stigma associated with demotions and reductions in responsibilities. Employees in American business organizations are oriented to career *advancement*, with the implication that advancement means bigger not smaller job assignments. To make flexible retirement policies work effectively, therefore, the attitude toward lateral or downward career moves needs to be positive. Management policy statements are helpful, but most helpful are specific successful examples of such job modifications. By making such changes reality, they may become part of the way of life.

Finally, special job assignments are often used as a technique for moving older individuals away from their regular jobs and into temporary assignments that can utilize their talents while unblocking career paths in an organization. Sometimes this is interpreted as "shelving undesirables" or creating an "executive attic." To many, it means finding or creating jobs for deadwood. Such interpretations are unfortunate, because companies regularly have short-term projects such as plant start-ups, special study projects, training programs, and planning projects that require experienced talent. Such temporary assignments, which may range from 2 months to 2 years, encourage older employees to reevaluate personal interests and plans, to consider alternative career opportunities, and to consider the attractiveness of retirement. Special assignments may be a gentle nudge toward the retirement door, or they may, in practice, be valuable and satisfying work experiences that tap senior employees' specialized skills and experience.

TERMINATIONS

A fourth course for flexible retirement is termination. Not retirement, but termination—severance for good cause. Some employees wish to continue working but are not performing adequately by management standards. If they cannot be induced to retire early and if the alternatives of gradual retirement, career change, or job modification are not accept-

able, management may act to move them out of the organization.

As discussed earlier, terminations may not be based on
age and must be substantiated by evidence of inadequate
performance relative to established job standards or objectives. With the new Federal Age Act amendments, this is the
only way employees may be forced out. If they are eligible
for retirement benefits, such terminations may be considered
"forced" retirements by the affected employees. Hence terminations represent a tool of management to implement
"flexible" retirement policies and are discussed further in
Chapter 9.

EXPERIENCE WITH FLEXIBLE RETIREMENT

Some of these techniques may seem unconventional, but all
have been applied successfully by employers. All are potentially useful means of introducing more flexible retirement
arrangements, allowing older employees to continue working
in a manner that fits their abilities and interests as well as the
company's needs. When applied, these techniques become
accepted practical aspects of management practices.

A number of corporations have operated without a mandatory retirement age and have gotten along satisfactorily.
Among these are Bankers Life & Casualty Insurance Company, Walt Disney Studios, Paddock Publications, U.S. Steel
(hourly and nonmanagerial salaried employees), Connecticut General Life Insurance Company, and Tektronix. At
Bankers Life, 25% of the employees are over the age of 50
and less than 4% over the age of 65. These proportions have
remained virtually unchanged since 1954, when the policy
was adopted. Additionally, the federal government has operated with an age-70 limit without apparent adverse effects.
Reportedly fewer than 3000 employees stay on to that age
each year. The state governments of Illinois, Florida, and

Pennsylvania function without any mandatory retirement age.

Various of the flexible retirement techniques discussed in this chapter have been applied in these organizations. And they have also been applied in other organizations to ease the application of age-65 or earlier retirement.

THE IMPACT

Because a large proportion of employees are opting to retire early and because many feel that the traditional retirement age of 65 is "normal," the actual number of cases that need to be handled under a flexible retirement program may be extremely small. In one large company's analysis of the impact of a mandatory retirement ban, the number of prospectively affected employees was found to be fewer than 100 a year. Of nearly 1000 employees becoming eligible for retirement, two-thirds were expected to retire prior to 65 and a majority of the remainder to leave at 65, voluntarily. It was felt that these individual cases could be effectively handled through counseling and application of flexible retirement techniques.

Even as the number of prospective retirees grows during the next two decades, most employees will find retirement timing that suits their personal needs and circumstances. Most executives agree that individuals generally know what their abilities and interests are. The cases where "Old Joe has been hanging on for years" are relatively few and will likely become more rare as companies adopt more objective performance evaluations and more extensive flexible retirement arrangements. The emerging generation of older workers tends to be more affluent, more conscious of the factors involved in career and retirement planning, and more likely to make the adjustment easily without relying on forced retirement.

CHAPTER FIVE

INDUCING EARLY RETIREMENTS

Our policy of normal retirement at age 60 has been an important ingredient of our success over the years. In addition to assuring future promotional opportunities on a predictable basis, especially for management positions, it has seemed to meet the needs and preferences of most employees—A company president.

During the past few years attitudes toward retirement in general and early retirement in particular have shifted considerably. Retirement was once thought of as a conclusion and early retirement as a rejection (often equivalent to a firing). Retirement is now widely viewed as a desirable objective, opening up new forms of activity and productivity. A major factor in the changed attitude has been the increasingly adequate financial protection available to retirees. Improved private pension plan benefits, increased Social Security and Medicare program benefits, as well as greater personal wealth have all accelerated the movement toward early retirement.

With the raising of mandatory retirement age and the ultimate end of mandatory retirement, employers instinctively turn to retirement benefits improvement as a key to inducing early retirements. In response to the 1978 amendments, many

companies will likely expand and enrich their early retirement programs. This chapter discusses the several forms
early retirement inducements may take.

30 AND OUT

Credit for the development and widespread acceptance of
early retirement programs is often attributed to the labor
unions who negotiated such provisions in the 1960s. With
the primary aim of providing opportunity for younger workers, unions have pushed for benefits that made the prospect
of voluntary retirement attractive. In 1966 the steelworkers
negotiated the first "30 and out" provision. The provision
enabled employees to retire once 30 years of service were
put in, regardless of age. Previously both years of service and
a minimum age (55 or 60) were required.

Under the provision, which has been negotiated for many
employees by the United Auto Workers, United Rubber
Workers, Electrical Workers, and others, early retirement has
become a way of life. Basic retirement benefits are supplemented under the plans to make up for loss of Social Security
benefits in instances where workers retire before eligibility.
For example, rubber workers receive a flat $200 each month
as a supplement to their pension until they reach age 62,
when they start receiving Social Security benefits. Also, most
of the plans specify automatic cost-of-living adjustments to
make up for the loss of pension buying power in times of
inflation.

SALARIED AND MANAGERIAL
EMPLOYEE PLANS

Few companies have comparable programs for salaried employees, but many have taken steps to liberalize pension
eligibility and the benefits provided prior to "normal" retire-

ment age. Experience has indicated that blue-collar workers are anxious to retire—to get away from their jobs. Generally, salaried and managerial workers look forward to retirement as a phase of life, not as relief from work. The jobs, as a rule, are an important source of personal recognition and satisfaction. To be willing to give them up requires a strong retirement incentive. The focus in this chapter, then, is on inducements tailored to these employee groups.

BASIC EARLY RETIREMENT PROVISIONS

The first step taken was to allow early retirements under pension plans that specified a normal retirement age. If employees wished to retire early, they could begin receiving their accrued pension immediately, but at the actuarial equivalent value of their normal pension. The monthly benefits would be reduced (usually by approximately 6%) to allow for the fact that contributions to the plan on their behalf would be made for fewer years and that the payment of benefits would be for more years than if they had retired at the "normal" age.

Thus this initial change did not cost employers anything, and the reduction was so great that few employees were interested in retiring early. In addition to the reduced pension, employees correctly observed that if they stayed to normal retirement the salary base on which the pensions are calculated might be greater, meaning a larger pension benefit.

In the 1960s, however, many employers liberalized the provisions for early retirement. First, they eased the percentage reduction to lessen the shrinkage of monthly pension benefits and in some cases eliminated the reduction entirely to, say, the age of 62 or 60. Second, they provided "make-up to Social Security" as described above, for those employees who retired prior to the age of 62 and were not yet eligible for Social Security benefits.

In 1961 only 16% of 841 pension plans surveyed by the Conference Board provided for liberalized early retirement benefits, although 90% had early retirmeent provisions based on an actuarial discount. By 1971 some 30% had liberalized provisions (Meyer and Fox, 1971). Practically all the growth came through plans that provided a liberalized benefit to *all* employees who met the regular early retirement eligibility requirements. In a sense, the liberalization of salaried plans followed the precedent established for negotiated plans. Today the pension plans of major employers feature a liberalized early retirement provision and a majority of retirees take advantage of it by retiring early, as opposed to only 5% in 1971 and 2% in 1961 (Meyer and Fox, 1971, p. 39).

Basic retirement benefit plans may be modified in three areas, therefore, in support of flexible retirement arrangements:

- A liberalized early retirement discount which reduces the accrued benefit for each year the employee is under the age of 65 (or the normal retirement age specified in the benefit plans). For example, an individual retiring at the age of 60 is actuarially entitled to 67% of the pension that would be paid at the age of 65; a liberalized early retirement provision would pay 85%.

- A full retirement benefit is paid without discount after a specified age, say, 60 or 62. Such programs generally have a substantial service requirement (e.g., 25 years) or an age-and-service combination formula (e.g., totaling 80).

- A supplemental benefit is paid to make up for Social Security benefits until the early retirees become eligible for these benefits.

EXAMPLES

Two case examples illustrate liberalized early retirement provisions in company retirement benefit plans.

First, a large East Coast bank allows unreduced retirement benefits to employees at the age of 60 with 15 years' service. The normal retirement age is 65. The plan pays 1½% of average annual earnings (basic compensation) during the individual's 5 highest paid consecutive years of the last 10 years' service times the number of years of plan participation up to 40 years. Early retirement is allowed as early as 55, with an actuarially reduced benefit.

A major oil company allows retirement at any age between 50 and 65 if age plus service equals or exceeds 75. The pension benefit is 2% multiplied by years of service (maximum 35) multiplied by average final earnings (best consecutive 5 of 10 years). In this case the pension is also indexed for increases in cost of living, according to the Consumer Price Index (maximum 10%).

In both plans there are offsets for Social Security benefits; that is, the total pension benefit represents the combined benefits received from the company plan and from Social Security (once the retiree is eligible).

SPECIAL PROGRAMS

Early retirement provisions in basic pension plans may not be adequate incentives for voluntary early retirement. If companies wish to induce early retirements, special programs are needed. Such programs are typically supplemental to retirement benefit plans and are temporary in nature. In fact, it is important to assure they are not construed as retirement benefits, for if they are they may fall under ERISA (Employee Retirement Income Security Act) regulations regarding funding, reporting, and disclosure.

Companies introduce special early retirement programs for various reasons, including:

■ To reduce overall staffing levels.

■ To create opportunities for new talent to assume key job responsibilities.

■ To create promotional opportunities (through a chain effect of replacements) and entry-level hiring vacancies.

■ To provide competitive compensation features (to maintain image of being progressive).

Some companies also believe that induced early retirements reduce overall compensation costs by substituting less costly (younger) talent for older senior talent. However, this belief is often invalid, because costs rise as employees are advanced to fill the vacated positions.

There is a fine line between a special early retirement program and a short-term severance program. The key differences are the eligibility of individuals for participation (an age and service requirement), the fact that early retirement is voluntary, and the intention of making early retirement a positive, attractive option (as opposed to the negative view of severance or termination programs). In Chapter 9 termination programs and practices are discussed as tools for forcing declining performers to leave the company. Whether an employee leaves under a special retirement program or a severance arrangement, the potential for age discrimination is present, and care should be exercised by management to minimize this risk. The emphasis in early retirement is on the voluntary nature of the individual's decision; in termination programs the emphasis is on management documentation of evaluated performance and capabilities relative to valid standards.

Special programs are formal, temporary provisions enabling a designated group of eligible employees to elect voluntary early retirement. For example, in 1971 Eastman

Kodak offered a program to induce early retirements. Any employee at least 55 years old who retired with the company's consent between September 1 and December 1 was paid the full amount of pension benefits accrued to retirement date and a supplement of $200 a month to age 62 or 65. Employees aged 55 had to have 30 years of service to qualify. For each year over that age the service requirement was cut 2 years.

IBM offered a special program in 1971 and again in 1975. Employees with 25 years of service were offered a bonus of 2 years' salary payable over a 4-year period if they would leave IBM. This bonus was in addition to regular accrued retirement benefits. Each program was extended for 6 months' time only. Of the eligible employees, one in three accepted in 1971; one in four in 1975.

Special programs may take the form of a temporary retirement income supplement, a lump sum bonus, a bonus paid in installments, or other payments, usually representing an allowance based on pay. The form, then, is similar to a severance benefit, but it is extended as an incentive for voluntary early retirement. In many special programs, companies also extend certain employee benefits (medical, insurance, etc.) until regular retirement age.

Under such special programs, there is the risk that the "good" performers will leave and the less desirable performers will stay. The experience of companies having such programs has indicated that many talented employees do, in fact, take advantage of the program. Many of these take postretirement positions with other companies, often competitors. However, many poor performers also leave; thus the loss of good talent is simply a price to be paid. It has been observed that well-managed companies have a depth of talent, and good people promptly rise to fill the gaps. Similarly, it has been observed that it takes a strong organization to be able to initiate such a program.

SELECTIVE INDUCEMENTS

Fearing that the company may lose needed skills and good performers, early retirement inducements are often offered on an individualized basis. These early retirements may be considered "negotiated retirements" or simply "payoffs" for people to leave voluntarily. The aim is to induce specific individuals to leave, under the umbrella of "early retirement," in a manner that is satisfactory to both the affected individuals and the company.

Salary continuation for a year or 18 months is the most common form of arrangement. A form of severance pay, employees receive this compensation in addition to any accrued retirement benefits. Most importantly, however, is that individuals can say that they have voluntarily retired early. Personal pride as well as financial reward have been recognized. Typically, such arrangements are made only when a person is blocking a career path or is no longer making a significant contribution to the organization. As organizations change and demands grow, older professionals and managers frequently have difficulty adapting to new challenges and requirements. Special early retirement inducements allow these individuals to retire under terms that are personally favorable.

In practice, selective inducements are poorly disguised terminations. In an insurance company, for example, employees selected to be "encouraged" to retire early are given 1 year's notice. Their compensation is the year's pay, which they receive whether they stay on the job for the year or leave promptly. If the inducement is a threat of termination, great care should be taken to help the individuals reach their own career decisions voluntarily. Positive employee attitudes are sought through the use of the tool; otherwise, outright termination procedures are more appropriately applied.

Thus counseling and a great deal of positive support and encouragement by managers and peers are needed to help affected individuals retire with a smile.

Obviously, individuals may decline the offer of early retirement. Employers who appear to be coercing individuals to retire early are guilty of forcing retirements, which is illegal under the law. Employees may be adversely treated in their jobs to the extent that they welcome an option to retire early under a special arrangement, but such adverse treatment on the job may be considered discrimination based on age. Special inducements must be just that—inducements—and not subterfuges for dismissals.

In some companies senior professionals and managers are offered consulting arrangements as part of special early retirement packages. These ease the transition for the individuals and assure the company that needed skills and knowledge will be available should they be needed. However, companies must be careful to offer consulting arrangements only when consulting is actually contemplated. Under IRS regulations, such compensation is tax deductible only if it is for services performed. Thus if consulting is not what is wanted, but rather departure by the individuals, a simpler severence or lump sum arrangement is advisable.

More than half of 800 companies surveyed by the Conference Board in 1977 reported that they will rehire employees who had already retired. Of course, under the law, companies are required to consider retirees under the age of 70 as job applicants on equal terms with other applicants. But retirement employment may serve as an inducement to individuals to retire early. And some employees will become very effective performers when working on a part-time basis or on different jobs more suited to their skills and abilities. The lure of postretirement employment brings a promise of both additional retirement income and the chance to remain as part of the organization.

SPECIAL PROGRAMS FOR EXECUTIVES

In testifying at hearings on the recent federal legislation, company spokesmen indicated that mandatory retirement was particularly necessary to force executives to retire. Without an age ceiling, executives will tend to hang on, limiting career opportunities for others and potentially hampering progress and lowering the effectiveness of management. Accordingly, there was included in the law an executive exemption for highly paid executives with annual retirement benefits of $27,000 or more. These individuals may be forced to retire at 65.

Yet the need remains for companies to provide inducements for executives to retire early. As a rule, executives tend to retire early anyway. A TPF&C study of executive retirements in 27 major companies indicated that over half retire early. In the survey group, 75% retired substantially early, at a median age of 63.

Basic pension plan provisions discussed above apply, of course, to executives as well as to other employee groups. However, many companies also rely on special inducements to encourage selected executives to retire, and from time to time some companies establish temporary "open window" retirement programs for the executive group. Most arrangements are informal and discretionary, although some companies have formal plans providing for special treatment of executives at early retirement. In some, compensation levels are specified (e.g., 75% of pay); in others they are not mentioned. Of the formal plans used, typical approaches are lump sum payments up to 2 years' salary based on level and years of service, preretirement leaves of absence of up to a year on full pay, and specially arranged deferred pension supplements (annuities).

The informal nature of executive-level inducements is due

to the feeling that each individual has different objectives and needs. Some compensation is probably required to make the executive "indifferent" to either retiring or continuing to work. Or, perhaps, a slightly larger amount is needed to tip the balance in favor of retirement. In most cases the amount of compensation for executive early retirement is generous. A company that has consistently offered 2 years' salary (maximum) to encourage early retirements has been highly successful. Thus the balance of benefits combined with the executive's feelings and attitudes toward early retirement make very little other incentive necessary to stimulate the early retirement decision.

Formal executive retirement plans are typically written, nonqualified (under IRS regulations, they must be paid for from current annual earnings), and are not prefunded. They define the eligibility requirements (including definition of an executive), the normal retirement benefit, the early retirement benefit, the spouse's benefit, and the vesting requirement. It is, therefore, a special plan for retirement income designed and administered for a small executive group, apart from other employee benefit plans.

Over the years formal plans have become more common as companies wish to standardize the treatment of executives and to disclose matters of executive compensation in proxies and other documents. This does not mean that informal inducements are not being used. Both forms are applied, in some intances in combination.

CHAPTER SIX

CONTROLLING RETIREMENT COSTS

Even companies which defended mandatory retirement . . . conceded that the
economic impact of a ban on mandatory retirement would be negligible for
them. . . . A spokesperson noted that it
may well cost the company more to pay
the older worker's pension benefits and
to pay the salary of his replacement than
it would cost to retain the worker beyond the mandated age of retirement—
*Mandatory Retirement: The Social and
Human Cost of Enforced Idleness.*

Proponents of maintaining a mandatory retirement age of 65
have argued that this policy has helped companies plan for
personnel needs and control personnel costs. With a higher
age limit, or no limit at all, costs would certainly rise because
of higher salary costs of older employees, higher medical and
life insurance costs, and reduced productivity. Further, they
argue, management would be less able to predict and control
retirement costs because of the uncertain timing of retirements by individual employees. An older work force, in
summary, is a more costly work force.

Allaying these concerns, Congressmen indicated in the

House Committee Hearings in 1977 that the act was intended to cover employment practices, not employee benefit plans. Improvements in benefits, continuation of accruals beyond "normal retirement age," or increases in pension benefits actuarially after actual retirement would not be required under the act. Presumably, a plan may provide that employees receive the same benefit on actual retirement that they would have received had they retired at normal retirement age. Therefore, to the extent that retirement is postponed and the ultimate benefit remains the same, the cost of the retirement plan is actually reduced. The bill does not appear to ban the practice of reducing coverage (or increasing employee cost for maintaining coverage) in benefit programs as age increases. A plan could reduce or eliminate life insurance coverage for an employee who reaches a specified age. Similarly, a plan could require that employees increase their contributions per $1000 of life insurance coverage as age increases.

The immediate cost impact of the law may be inconsequential. There are cost implications in areas other than employee benefits, among them training, recruiting, changes in salary costs, and patterns of employee productivity and absenteeism. This chapter examines these potential aspects of increased costs and cost savings relating to the end of mandatory retirement.

At the same time, it would be naive to plan only modifications in plans and practices in anticipation of a retirement age of 70. Clearly, the proponents of retirement age legislation at state and federal levels are interested in elimination of age as a factor in employment. Differential benefits related to age would be unacceptable without demonstration by the employer of economic hardship. One way or another, extension of full benefits will likely be required after the age of 65, and employers will have very little to say about when an employee retires. Pressures are growing via the human rights movement for equal treatment in all aspects of employment, and this aspect is now a highly visible and controversial one.

Finally, as discussed in the last chapter, costs may rise as benefits are improved to induce voluntary retirements. Employees, not the employers, have the option to continue employment status. The employers must persuade employees that it is more attractive to retire than to continue working. And this means costly improvements in benefits and related programs discussed in this book. Of course, the extent of these costs depends on the adequacy of present programs.

WHAT COSTS ARE INVOLVED?

For most employers, the immediate question that came to mind when word of the law's passage arrived was: "How much will this add to our employee benefit program costs?" Because benefit costs are substantial and are formalized in plan documents and periodic cost evaluations, they are first and foremost in management consideration. But, as noted, there may be some offsetting cost savings, at least for the immediate term, as employees defer retirement timing.

Additionally, there are other potential costs and offsetting cost savings associated with early or late retirement timing. Among these are recruitment and training expenditures, salary, and expenses associated with productivity changes as older employees stay on longer. A flexible retirement policy introduces a multiplicity of costs and benefits which need to be considered by management.

Figure 1 indicates areas of potentially increased costs and cost savings associated with early retirement and deferred retirement. As shown, early retirement programs bear additional costs to an employer, whether resulting from basic benefit improvements or special programs. Also, early retirements result in costs associated with the recruitment and

Retirement Timing	Early	Later
Potentially increased costs	Retirement benefits	Higher salaries
	Recruitment and training of replacements	Certain employee benefit costs (medical, insurance)
		Productivity decline because of vacations, illness, obsolescence, etc.
Potential cost savings	Replacement by younger, lower-paid employees	Reduced recruitment and training costs
	Reduction in the number of positions	Lower retirement benefit costs
		Reduced absenteeism
		Strong work motivation

Figure 1. Employer Costs and Cost Savings.

training of replacements. Certain cost savings are widely believed to result from early retirements: reduction of salary by replacement of older employees with lesser-paid employees and the overall reduction of staffing levels. In fact, these two cost savings were the motivation for many special early retirement programs introduced by companies in the 1960s and early 1970s. While some savings were attained through early retirement programs, many companies found that salaries soon rose (because the positions, not the people, are the basis of job evaluation systems) and that staffing soon crept back up when economic pressures eased. It is ironic that such efforts to reduce costs through early retirements was one factor impelling the passage of legislation banning age discrimination. Public sentiment against forced early retirements was aroused by news accounts of company actions and reinforced by court decisions that either said such actions were allowable or cited them as age discrimination.

Of course, an important reason for offering early retirement programs is not directly cost related, but rather related to a qualitative improvement in management effectiveness. If sales are increased, if research is more creative, and if individual managers are more energetic and competitive, the argument goes, the benefits of early retirement programs far exceed the costs.

Later retirement also bears potentially increased costs: higher salary costs associated with length of service and organizational level, higher benefit costs associated with age, and reduced productivity (in the broad sense) because of increased vacations and frequency of illness as well as diminished performance abilities. These costs are not universal, but they are commonly cited in arguments against later retirement ages. Salary costs and productivity costs need to be examined on a case-by-case basis; benefits costs are examined in this chapter in the light of legislated requirements.

Offsetting savings potentially include reduced recruitment and training costs by retention of qualified talent, decreased retirement benefit costs due to the deferral of payments and consequent shorter life expectancy, and improved productivity due to lower absenteeism and greater work motivation and commitment. Again, these savings vary with individuals and circumstances, but the factors need to be taken into consideration. In the Congressional hearings, many company spokespersons acknowledged that company benefits and broader social benefits attained through later retirement would exceed any associated costs.

The nature of costs and cost savings depends on individuals and on company circumstances. Many of the fears voiced regarding the end of mandatory retirement centered on increased costs and loss of managerial control over staffing and performance. The experience of companies that have operated without mandatory retirement, however, has indicated that many fears are unfounded:

- Few employees wish to work beyond the age of 70, or even 65.

- Even fewer employees desire to be retrained or reassigned late in their careers.

- Accident and illness rates, as well as overall absenteeism tend to be lower, not higher, for older employees.

- High salary costs of older employees are offset by the costs of recruiting and training new younger workers.

A spokesperson for CBS noted that it may well cost a company more to pay the older worker's pension benefits and to pay the salary of his replacement than it would cost to retain the worker beyond the mandated age of retirement (Select Committee on Aging, 1977, p. 36). The companies that defended mandatory retirement before the House committee conceded that the economic impact of a ban on mandatory retirement would be negligible for them. The representative from General Motors, for one, testified that retaining those who wanted to remain after its age of mandatory retirement would not create an economic problem. Numerous other companies apparently decided not to testify after examining the cost factors and likely number of employees that would stay on in their organizations. The principal concern among employers, noted earlier in this chapter, was with increased benefits costs for employees over the age of 65.

BENEFITS IMPLICATIONS

In the private nonfarm sector of United States employment, 40 million persons participate in private pension plans. Most of these plans have a normal retirement age of 65. According

to a 1974 Department of Labor study, of 20.6 million partici-
pants in defined benefit plans, 41% were covered by mandatory retirement age provisions, usually 65, the same as the
normal retirement age. Another 10% belonged to plans that
had forced early retirement provisions, under which a worker
could be compelled to retire before the age of 65. Such age
provisions were found in about 50% of the nonnegotiated
plans and in about 40% of those plans negotiated with unions.
The provisions were common in all types of industries.

For many employee benefit plans, therefore, the age of
65 has been an important benchmark. The amount of pension
is calculated on the assumption it will begin at this age. No
further pension recognition is usually given employment
after 65. And even though the pension would not begin until
actual retirement if a worker stays beyond the age of 65, the
pension does not usually reflect any upward adjustment for
the longer service and later starting date.

Of the companies that have age-65-oriented plans, there
are evidently two groups: those that wish to stay that way to
the extent allowable within the law and those that would like
to adopt changes in support of more flexible retirement. Improvements in benefits coverages for older employees and
for retirees incur additional costs for employers. Hence, consideration of the expected benefits and benefits-costs implications of age discrimination law is necessary for both of these
groups of companies.

There is a third group of companies: those that have no
mandatory retirement age and have, in general, attempted to
treat employees at all ages equally. Here the end of mandatory retirement has little meaning, from a legal impact perspective. Most of these companies, as noted, have few employees retiring at the age of 65 or later; thus they have
found the liberal policy to be relatively easy to administer
and without burdensome costs.

The following sections discuss the expected implications

of the 1978 amendments and a future ban on mandatory retirement at any age for specific groups of benefits: pensions, thrift and profit sharing plans, medical plans, disability, and death.

PENSIONS

The Federal bills as drafted indicate no real intent to extend benefits beyond the age of 65. Nor was their any intent to modify (or create any conflicts with) ERISA. Accordingly, the original interpretation of the act was that the short-term effects would be generally inconsequential.

To clarify the benefits implications of the proposed law, Senators Javits (New York) and Williams (New Jersey) posed several key questions to the Department of Labor. Briefly, the questions and the responses were as follows:

Q: Would an employer be required to credit years of service for purposes of benefit accrual after normal retirement age?

A: Nothing in the ADEA or in the proposed amendments would require an employer to credit, for purposes of benefit accrual those years of service which occur after an employee's normal retirement age. (ERISA explicitly permits a plan to provide that no benefits will accrue after normal retirement age.)

Q: Would an employer be required to pay the actuarial equivalent of normal retirement benefits to an employee who continues to work beyond the normal retirement age?

A: No. There will not have to be any adjustment in the size of the periodic payments at the time of actual retirement.

Q: Could plans that specify commencement of retirement benefits at age 65 be amended to provide that benefits would commence at the actual date of retirement without violating the ADEA or ERISA?

A: ERISA requires that benefits commence at normal retirement age or on the actual date of retirement, whichever is later. If there are some plans which provide for the payment of pension benefits at a specified age, regardless of actual retirement, such plans could be amended without violating the ADEA or ERISA.

Q: Would an increase in the upper age limit of the ADEA increase the funding costs for private pension plans?

A: No. As a matter of fact, financial pressure on private pension plans could be alleviated. As an actuarial matter, the longer an employee works, the shorter the period retirement payments will have to be made, thus lowering the funding assumptions of the plan. Savings, of course, would come from the added years of accumulated interest on the fund. Savings would also stem from the fact that a plan need not provide for further accrual of benefits after normal retirement age and thus the added years of service do not increase the ultimate benefit or the cost of providing it. Any increases in benefits due to such factors as salary increases after normal retirement age would be offset by factors such as the shorter life expectancy of employees, interest earned on plan assets, and pre-retirement mortality.

Q: Would an employer's failure to provide for the accrual of benefits after normal retirement age constitute age discrimination under the ADEA?

A: A bona fide pension plan that provides that no benefits accrue to a participant who continues service with the employer after normal retirement age would not violate the ADEA. The legislative history of the ADEA indicates that Section 4(f)(2) was intended to allow age to be considered in funding a plan and in determining the level of benefits to be paid.

Department of Labor regulations interpreting the 1967 ADEA indicated that an employer is not required to provide older employees with the same pension, retirement, or insurance benefits as are provided the younger employees, so long as the differential is in accordance with the terms of a bona fide employee benefit plan. For example, a plan will be considered in compliance if the cost incurred on behalf of an older worker is equal to that incurred on behalf of a younger worker, even though the older worker may receive lesser benefits. The raising of the protected age from 65 to 70 merely expands the group covered.

For an employer who presently recognizes postnormal retirement age service and wishes to eliminate such accrual, there are several possible obstacles. A claim of age discrimination could be made. An amendment to a plan deleting such a provision might constitute a curtailment under IRS rules. Third, such an amendment might be prohibited as decreasing accrued benefits, unless carefully written. Thus employers who have offered such a benefit might find it hard to take it away, even though it is not required under the law.

Speaking for the joint committee of Congress that developed the final law, Representative Hawkins and Senator Williams also indicated that employers need not make contributions on behalf of employees working past the normal retirement date; contributory plans may also prohibit employee contributions after this date.

In defined contribution plans such as profit sharing and thrift plans which are supplemental, the 1967 ADEA and ERISA already require continued participation of employees within a protected class. If this is true and the class is expanded, then additional contributions and shorter life expectancy of employees who defer retirement will result in greater retirement income from such plans, assuming no significant investment losses.

LONG-TERM PENSION IMPLICATIONS

Although it is currently believed that use of age in determining pensions is legal, including "freezing" benefits at 65, companies should be prepared for the possibility that government will mandate "equal treatment" in benefits for all employees of all ages. Employee demands for fairness and nondiscriminatory treatment, the groundswell that led to the 1978 amendments, are likely to bring further changes. The 1978 changes represent merely a step toward total elimination of age as a factor in pension, retirement, and employment practices.

Equal treatment of over-65 employees may require continued benefit accruals with extended credited service and recognition of pay after the age of 65 as a basis of pension calculation. Recognition of pay after 65 alone might offset possible pension savings resulting from deferred retirements. Recognition of additional credited service may or may not have significant cost implications, depending on whether the pension plan formula gives full, reduced, or no credit for service after a certain period of years (e.g., 25 or 30 years' service). Additionally, it is possible that an employee's pension at 65 will have to be actuarially increased if retirement is deferred. This, of course, would be very expensive if compounded with the other projected changes. In summary, future pension benefits may very well be based solely on years of service rather than age.

MEDICAL, DISABILITY, AND OTHER BENEFITS

Other benefit plans are designed and costed with the premise of a work force under the age of 65. Simple facts of aging indicate that the risks of illness, disability, and death increase with age, and particularly after the age of 65.

Under the ADEA, as amended, employers are not required to provide to employees over 65 any benefits that are not now provided. However, it will soon become obvious to employees who elect to work beyond 65 that they are not getting their share of benefits coverage. In the long-term, then, companies will be compelled, probably by further legislation, to extend benefits coverage to workers who stay beyond the normal retirement age. Without defined limits, whether under federal or state laws, employers will need to modify their benefit plans and incur the additional costs associated with extended age coverages.

Many companies today provide employees over the age of 65 with a hospital, surgical, and medical benefit that supplements Medicare. The company plan coverage drops or is limited to filling the "holes" in Medicare. In the future, companies that drop all coverage after 65 will likely be forced to add some kind of plan to make up the difference between Medicare and company-sponsored coverage available to employees under 65. Full makeup will be expensive. And there is also the possibility that Medicare eligibility and benefits will be modified, creating a larger gap to be bridged for older employees.

The prevailing pattern in long-term disability plans is to provide coverage only up to the age of 65, regardless of employment. Extending the benefits beyond 65 could be costly. The incidence and duration of disability can be expected to increase for employees over 65. In fact, a permanently disabled employee might continue to receive disability benefits for life if there were no mandatory retirement age. Thus as an employee, a disabled person could "retire" with benefits under the disability plan greater than those provided by the retirement plan. An employee might be motivated to continue working until disabled (because of declining physical or mental capacities), so that the more adequate disability benefit could be received. This may be particularly logical for employees with shorter service and thus lesser pension benefit eligibility. The alternatives to employers include reducing long-term disability benefits and relating them to service (to the disadvantage of the young, short-service employee) or increasing pension disability benefits with comparable costs. With either form of improvement, disability insurance costs will surely rise: one insurance company has estimated increases in costs of 50%.

To cope with possible increases in illness among older workers, companies may wish to review their sick pay plans. Few statistics are available, but costs may increase 15% for sick pay plan (approved absences for illness) coverage for employees over the age of 65. Similarly, short-term disability plans will be used more commonly by older employees. Frequency, duration, and recurrence of use will increase. Either the costs must be borne or the overall plan modified.

GROUP LIFE INSURANCE

Under most benefit plans, death benefits are either eliminated or reduced immediately to a nominal amount at the age of 65, even if the individual remains employed. For example, an employee whose annual compensation is $20,000 might be covered for $40,000 of life insurance while employed before 65. On reaching that age (or retiring early), the amount of coverage might be reduced to 25% of full salary, or $5000. This practice arose because the cost of providing insurance rises dramatically after the age of 55. Even a modest amount of insurance can be costly, since a "claim" is a certainty at some point.

The continuation of full insurance coverage for active employees over 65 could be extremely expensive. Nevertheless, future laws and regulations will likely require benefits to continue. This will impel employers to reconsider death benefits given all employees and to consider the total combination of death benefits provided: group life insurance, accident insurance, spouse's benefits, Social Security death benefits, and death benefits from profit sharing and thrift plans. Benefits from profit sharing and thrift plans tend to increase as the employee gets older. And, of course, Social Security kicks in greater benefits. Hence it would be logical to consider the targets or objectives of life insurance protection and develop a more comprehensive, rational plan that might place less emphasis on group insurance and more emphasis on survivors' income benefits.

It has been noted that if full insurance benefits are offered to older employees, there may again be an incentive to continue working because the benefits are "so good."

SOCIAL SECURITY COSTS

It should be noted that Social Security taxes will continue, and to the extent that older employees receive higher pay than the employees who would have replaced them, total Social Security costs to employers will be higher.

BENEFITS ADEQUACY

Regardless of legal requirements, employers may find they need to improve retirement benefits to induce employees over the age of 65 to retire voluntarily. In the view of many employees, income adequacy is a key test in the decision of when to retire (see Chapter 12). Benefits were once viewed as an employer gratuity to employees for long service. Then they became considered part of earned compensation (hence the concern with vesting and pension "rights"). Now, it appears that retirement benefits will become a necessary management tool to induce retirement. Companies will need to determine carefully or reconsider the objectives of retirement benefit plans, so that the costs expended will serve defined aims.

Also, there is the problem of inflation. Employees may be hesitant to retire in the face of rapid inflation that brings with it eroding retirement income. Pension plans will have to address the question of postretirement adjustments for inflation in a more systematic way if this concern is to be allayed. Periodic gratuitous increases in pensions generally are not an adequate inducement to retire when inflation is rampant.

Overall, it is safe to conclude that companies should assure that retirement benefits are adequate. Employees are not likely to retire if, in their judgment, benefits are insufficient. To make flexible retirement work in an age of no mandatory retirement, employers will need to offer a balanced and adequate retirement income package to induce employee retirement. This should include all income sources—pensions, profit sharing and thrift plans, and Social Security.

The costs of providing attractive retirement benefits are but one aspect of the overall costs relating to retirement. As discussed in this chapter, the indirect costs and benefits are far more significant, as a rule, than the highly visible out-of-pocket costs incurred in relation to benefit programs. Yet benefits are, in fact, highly visible, and for this reason they warrant priority consideration by employers in reviewing retirement policies and practices.

PART THREE

APPRAISING THE OLDER EMPLOYEE

CHAPTER SEVEN

APPRAISING PERFORMANCE AND ABILITY TO WORK

Why, when administrators must every day evaluate the competency of the younger worker, does that task become so onerous when the worker reaches age 65?—The Honorable Claude Pepper.

Most employers today have some kind of systematic performance appraisal program. Managers widely acknowledge that evaluation of individual employee performance and competence is an important aspect of good personnel management. They use appraisal information in making personnel decisions concerning promotions, compensation, layoffs, terminations, demotions, training, and other terms and conditions of employment. Factors other than performance or merit are sometimes considered, but most managers would agree that appraisals are important.

In many instances, however, performance appraisals are conducted informally and are not directly related to specific job requirements. Appraisals are often hastily prepared and reflect only general impressions of individual performance. They often reflect subjective opinions of appraisers and focus on personal characteristics of the individuals appraised rather than on actual job performance. If appraisals are general, informal, and subjective, there is a risk of age bias—of the appraisers making evaluations on the basis of age, not performance.

Pressures for more objective performance appraisals have been experienced by employers from equal opportunity laws. Court decisions have repeatedly indicated that a defensible appraisal system, free of bias, is important to support personnel actions having an adverse effect on women and minority employee groups (Basnight and Wolkinson, 1977; Holley and Feild, 1975). As a result, many companies have reviewed and strengthened their appraisal systems.

Perhaps more significant than the equal employment opportunity pressures will be the pressures brought to bear on employers by age discrimination law. Generally, employers have tended to give closer attention in appraisals to younger employees, as a basis for monitoring and guiding career progress. In many companies older employees are allowed to "coast" until retirement or until business conditions necessitate a reduction in staffing.

Court decisions in recent age discrimination cases, discussed in Chapter 3, indicate to employers that accurate and substantiated evidence of individual performance (and ability to perform) is necessary as a basis for justifying personnel actions that adversely affect protected older workers. With the raising or elimination of the mandatory retirement age, employers will bear an even greater responsibility for appraisals in rationalizing treatment of employees over the age of 65.

This chapter reviews current appraisal practices in light of the law and offers guidelines to employers for designing and applying performance appraisal programs.

APPRAISAL PRACTICES

Employers use various forms of performance appraisal. Figure 1 outlines the principal techniques for appraisal and experiences that employers have generally had with each.

There is no consensus among employers regarding the best approach, nor an approach that is most effective for minimizing possible age bias. Each has certain advantages and limitations that must be weighed before selecting a technique.

The difficulty of applying effective performance appraisal techniques was highlighted in a recent survey of 25 companies by the Conference Board (Lazer and Wikstrom, 1977). The survey identified numerous problems experienced in the use of performance appraisals. These include the following:

- Conflicting multiple uses.
- Unclear purpose or reasons for the program.
- Ratings biased by pay considerations.
- Lack of clear performance standards or criteria.
- Reliance on ratings of personality rather than performance.
- Biases such as halo persistence in ratings.
- Managers untrained to administer appraisals.
- Managers who dislike to give feedback to employees on appraisals.
- Conflicting coach and evaluator roles of managers.
- Appraisals that are viewed as administrative chore unrelated to business goals.
- The fact that appraisals are not used by top management.

Nevertheless, about two of three of the appraisal programs described in the survey were thought by the employers to be effective; that is, the programs were considered to be achieving the purposes for which they were designed. Whether the programs involve any discrimination on the basis of age was apparently not considered as a specific criterion.

The problems of appraisals noted above are the same as those that tend to create age discrimination problems. An ap-

Technique	Description	Advantages and Limitations
Narrative Appraisals Using job descriptions Role analysis Question/answer	Open-ended descriptions of individual performance	Flexible, allows rich detail if related to job requirements and standards Widely used, highly subjective
Goal Setting and Review Management by objectives (MBO) Budgets Direct measures of outputs of results	Establishment of goals and then comparison of performance against these goals	Flexible, allows participation by appraisee May not cover whole job, goals may change, standards may vary, evaluations may be highly subjective
Rating Scales Traditional Behaviorally anchored Q Sort	Performance evaluated against predetermined factors, on three, four, five, or more relative levels	Administratively convenient, easily tabulated and compared Relatively inflexible, quality depends on amount of work invested in scale building Ratings may be subjective usually no documentation of reasons for ratings
Checklists Task checklist List of qualities	Performance rated against list of normative factors	Applicable to clerical and other routine, task-defined jobs Simplicity may result in superficial appraisal
Critical Incidents	Examples of good and bad performance written down by ap-	Empirical, but tends to reflect only obvious performance incidents

Technique	Description	Advantages and Limitations
	praiser as they occur and retained for periodic review	Does not provide comparative appraisal basis
Ranking Traditional Multirater	Appraisers ranking subordinates by relative performance, either individually or by group consensus	Forces relative evaluation of performers, features multirater evaluations
		Lacks relevance to job standards, often highly subjective

Figure 1. Principal Techniques for Performance Appraisal.

praisal program designed to avoid the difficulties noted above will probably also avoid age discrimination problems. Or to put the point more positively, an appraisal program that is free of age bias is also one that serves well the needs of management in managing personnel.

DUAL PURPOSES OF APPRAISAL

One of the basic problems encountered by employers in appraising employee performance is the dual purpose of appraisals. On one hand, employers need objective evaluations of past individual performance for use in making personnel decisions. On the other hand, employers need tools to enable managers to help individuals improve performance, plan future work, develop skills and abilities for career growth, and strengthen the quality of their relationship as manager and employee.

Managers find it difficult to serve both as judge and counselor simultaneously—the dual roles required by these dual goals. When both purposes are served by one appraisal program, the results are often driven by salary administration needs. Justifying a given salary adjustment often overrides all other purposes of appraisals. Thus performance appraisal programs tend to be used for one or the other of these purposes, rarely for both.

As a result, many companies have separate appraisal programs for performance *evaluation* and performance *planning and review*. The former involves the manager's judgment of past performance for administrative decisions. The latter involves goal setting and review for future performance planning and employee development.

At Corning Glass Works, for example, the appraisal programs are structured so that employee evaluations are separate from goal setting sessions. In one interview a subordinate's performance, potential, promotability, and salary increase are discussed. The manager rates the individual's overall performance and potential. These ratings are shared with subordinates and endorsed by the supervisor at the next level. At another time, the manager discusses with the employee the performance goals and development plans achieved in the past period and planned for the future period.

A single appraisal system is rarely devised that can serve multiple purposes with ease. Some companies have concentrated on the goal setting (or MBO) process and have tried to stop evaluating performance as a separate aspect, but ultimately they have come back to doing both as separate, necessary programs (Patz, 1975).

The multifaceted aspects of appraisal, evaluation, and development, clearly require different characteristics to be effective. Figure 2 highlights the key differences in emphasis regarding purpose, focus, methods, responsibility, subject matter, and applications.

Because of the difficulty of objective evaluation and the more obvious payoff (and positive feelings) of developmen-

	Evaluation Approach	Development Approach
Purpose:	Assess past performance as a basis for personnel administration decisions	Motivate and direct individual performance and career development efforts
Focus:	Review of past	Planning for future
Method:	Judging Ratings/descriptions	Counseling/discussing Goal setting and review
Responsibility:	Manager as appraiser	Manager and employee share joint responsibility
Subject matter:	Past accomplishments	Future goals and plans
Applications:	Salary administration Transfers, promotions Layoffs, terminations Other personnel actions	Work planning Improving performance Developing capabilities Planning of training activities

Figure 2. Dual Approaches to Performance Appraisal.

tal performance planning and review, the trend in the past decade has been toward the developmental aspects (Thompson and Dalton, 1970). But now, with concern about possible age discrimination, together with possible race and sex discrimination, employers are giving the evaluation aspect of performance appraisal careful attention once again.

WHAT THE COURTS REQUIRE

Of the two aspects of performance appraisal, the law is concerned primarily with valid performance evaluation as the basis for personnel actions. Goal setting with employee participation may be viewed as a positive characteristic of an overall program, but it is not viewed as sufficient under the law. Evaluations must provide an accurate definition of individual performance in the organization relative to the actual meaning or standards of performance in the organization.

In practice, this means that employers need to design and implement appraisal programs that are *reasonable, relevant,* and *reliable*. These three key characteristics appear over and over again in judicial discussions of appraisals and their validity.

An appraisal program is reasonable if it generally is acceptable to its users. This means that the program is widely understood and supported as reasonably useful, necessary, fair, and as an objective process for evaluating (or rating) individual performance, with the purpose of the program clearly stated, and the procedures involved in the program having a minimum of vagueness. Employee participation in the design of the program and in subsequent reviews of its effectiveness are important. Communication of the purposes and elements of the program is essential (and often overlooked).

A program is relevant when it covers those aspects of work that are important and only those that are important. Relevance is assured by clear statements of job requirements and the kinds of on-the-job activities (behaviors) that are necessary for successful performance. Personality traits, race, sex, and age are rarely relevant to job performance. Thus the focus should be on how employees go about their work and the nature of outputs or results created. Chapter 8 discusses the techniques involved in defining the requirements and standards of job performance.

Appraisals are reliable when the results are reasonably free of significant defects. Evaluations of the same individual performance should be consistent among different raters and over time. They should contain a minimum of subjectivity that leads to distortion. Direct measures of output (units produced or sold) are the most reliable, but are not always identifiable. And so, ratings are often used as indirect measures and are highly dependent on the quality of information available about performance, on the ability of appraisers to make reliable judgments, and the use of consistent standards against which ratings are made.

For example, a technique of appraisal involving the use of behaviorally anchored scales is popular today because it scores high on all three of these criteria. An appraiser is required to select a point on each of a number of scales (e.g., 1–5) that fairly describes the observed performance of an individual employee. Each point on each scale is "anchored" to reality by a specific narrative description of a behavior or example of actual performance likely to be found in practice. The use of such scales is favored because: the realistic incidents built into the scales help ensure relevance, the anchored scales aiding consistent interpretation of performance help ensure reliability, and participation by employees and managers in developing the scales helps make them seem reasonable. However, the drawback of the technique is the high cost of developing and maintaining scales relevant to diverse and ever-changing jobs. Only large organizations, such as Sears, Roebuck and governmental organizations (including many police departments), have invested in this approach. Yet, in the final evaluation, the costs of such a rigorous technique must be weighed in light of potential company exposure to charges of unfair discrimination in appraising performance (Cheedle, Luthans, and Otteman, 1976).

GUIDELINES FOR PERFORMANCE APPRAISAL PROGRAMS

Any performance appraisal approach may be designed and applied in a manner that satisfies the foregoing basic requirements. In large measure, it is the manner of design and implementation that determines effectiveness of an appraisal program more than it is the particular set of techniques involved. Accordingly, the following guidelines focus upon the manner of designing and implementing performance appraisal programs.

1. Apply Specific Performance Standards. As is discussed in the next chapter, performance appraisals need to be based on specific, empirically derived job requirements. In many companies, job descriptions prepared for salary administration purposes serve as a starting point for performance evaluations. Too often they are the ending point as well, and appraisers are left to conceive applicable performance standards in the course of evaluating individual performance.

The Conference Board survey mentioned earlier found that only half the companies studied had analyzed the requirements of the positions covered by the appraisal systems. Companies are not accustomed to devoting time and resources to job analysis for purposes other than salary and wage administration. Some argue that goal setting techniques reduce the need for defined job standards, but these techniques appear to have little defense against charges of subjectivity and bias in appraisals.

The courts appear to require job performance standards that are based on some form of empirical analysis—examination of the actual job requirments as evidenced in practice. Interviews, questionnaires, observations, or other work analysis techniques may be used to provide empirical data on job-related performance requirements. The results need not be lengthy and detailed, but relevant aspects of performance need to be accurately identified and defined.

2. Assure that the Program Is Rationally Designed. The courts favor the view that a performance appraisal program should be rational. That is, the judge must feel that the system is designed for specific purposes that are reasonable and clearly identified and that the techniques adopted have the capacity to achieve these stated objectives.

The courts have not dictated what type of process or what techniques are the most acceptable. They have not dictated rules for the design of appraisal programs. It is incumbent on employers, then, to reconsider the multiple purposes being served by appraisals, to define carefully a philosophy and program (or programs) that effectively serve the objectives they have in mind.

Many companies, particularly large corporations, periodically review all appraisal programs being used and audit the results being obtained for them. Programs found deficient are overhauled; others are updated and reinforced for increased effectiveness. Different programs, involving various techniques, are commonly used in companies to meet diverse needs and circumstances.

3. Document Performance Evaluations.   Performance appraisals are often viewed as burdensome paperwork imposed by the personnel staff primarily for salary administration purposes. Although effective appraisals of performance need not involve any paperwork, the courts appear to feel that documentation is necessary, and written evaluations provide a company with a record of judgments underlying personnel actions.

An employer should obtain a written performance evaluation for each employee at least once a year. These evaluations should be retained for at least 3 years, even though the information may not be used in personnel decisions after the first year. The evaluations should reflect consideration of the performance requirements or standards and be consistent with the rationale of the overall appraisal program. They need not be lengthy (even one side of a page, handwritten, may suffice) as long as they are thoughtful and complete.

Summary ratings retained in manual or computer files are not sufficient, because they lack the detailed information revealing the judgments relating to job requirements. Summary ratings are useful for monitoring appraisal applications and rater consistency, and for examining patterns in employee performance among units or job categories. But ratings must be supplemental to more detailed narrative appraisals.

It should be noted that in some states employees have the right of access to these evaluation records. Statutes in California, Maine, and Oregon and pending laws in other states open the files to employees for information affecting their terms or conditions of employment. Because of these laws and a widespread employee interest in "privacy of data," at least half the Fortune 500 companies have instituted new policies covering employee access to their own personal records since 1975. Employers should develop and publish clear policies regarding employee access to appraisal records and be prepared to answer employee inquiries regarding their appraisals.

4. Administer the Program Systematically.   It is important for an employer to maintain a regular schedule for evaluations and to obtain complete participation by all appraisers. A hit-or-miss approach to appraisals simply does not get good results and does not show well in court. In many organizations evaluations are reviewed by managers one or more levels above the appraisers to assure proper administration of the program and to strengthen the objectivity of appraisals by introducing supplemental data and judgments. If some employees are given an opportunity to discuss their evaluations, either with appraisers or any of these other managers, the policy should apply to all.

In short, the courts require appraisal programs to display systematic procedures and policies of administration if they are to be used to defend an employer practice challenged as discriminatory. This reflects concern for equitable treatment of all groups of employees and a concern for regular, recurring appraisals as a matter of routine management practice. Ad hoc, haphazard appraisal programs do not carry much weight with the judges, nor with employees.

5. Train the Appraisers. Appraisal programs are often faulted because of inadequate appraiser skills. In many organizations managers have never been given training on how to conduct performance appraisals. If they have, the training typically involved only a brief orientation on the administrative procedures required by a new program, followed by periodic procedural memoranda or followup meetings.

Certainly, training should cover the administrative aspects of a program, including the forms, rating scales, use of standards and job requirements, linkages with salary administration, and timing. However, it should also help appraisers understand the objectives, problems, and behavioral aspects of performance evaluation and the parallel aspects of development and performance planning and review. Appraisers control the quality of appraisals, and need to be guided and motivated to give the program the necessary attention. Monitoring of appraisals by personnel staff can be useful in maintaining high-quality standards in appraisals, if the results of monitoring are communicated back to the appraisers. Conversely, appraisers can make valuable suggestions for the improvement of the program itself.

Above all, it is important that management support for appraisals be evident. In many companies the appraisal program begins with top management and cascades through the organization. The most powerful force in performance evaluation is the example of the appraiser's own manager as appraiser. Hence an ideal form of training is the proper use of the appraisal program itself, beginning with top managers appraising their direct subordinates.

CONCLUSION

The best performance appraisal program is one that works well. And this means that the program is reasonable, reliable, and relevant in design and application. The emphasis needs to be more on the use of the program by managers as appraisers than on a particular set of techniques or validation procedures. With the end of mandatory retirement, effective performance evaluations will be a management necessity.

CHAPTER EIGHT

DEFINING AGE-FREE JOB REQUIREMENTS

As the ADEA comes to be used increasingly, government, the courts and older workers themselves will insist that employers incorporate more objective . . . personnel selection, promotion, and termination procedures—Harold Sheppard and Sara Rix, *The Graying of Working America*, p. 79.

Definitions of job requirements have long been part of the personnel management "kit of tools." But only in recent years, with the advent of equal employment opportunity regulations and affirmative action programs have job requirements taken on significance as a basic tool for use in appraising performance, selecting and assigning employees, and terminations.

Under the ADEA, age may not be a factor in personnel actions adversely affecting the protected group of employees. Only in instances where age is demonstrated to be a bona fide occupational qualification (BFOQ) may employers refuse to hire or otherwise discriminate on the basis of age. Because individual differences in capabilities are so great, it is pretty difficult to prove that a given chronological age is a bona fide requirement.

In certain cases (e.g., particularly arduous law enforcement activity) there may be a factual basis for believing that most employees above a specified age would be unable to perform their jobs safely and efficiently, and such inability may prove impossible or impractical to determine through medical examinations and performance appraisals.

Nevertheless, many companies have taken the position that age is not a critical factor in defining job requirements, even though it has been present as a factor in past practice. AT&T, for example, has published a personnel policy to the effect that age is not to be considered a requirement for any position in the Bell System.

Age-free job requirements are necessary for flexible retirement practices. They can aid an employer in placing older workers on jobs suited to their capabilities, whether through recruitment, transfers, demotions, or other action. Additionally, they serve as the basis for performance appraisal—the standard by which individual employee performance is evaluated. And this means that job requirements indirectly affect termination decisions, salary actions, and various other personnel actions. They are the only possible replacement for managerial subjectivity in the necessary drive for objectivity in the treatment of employees. Job-related standards, as opposed to subjective personal standards, are essential for effective management and compliance with evolving employment law.

This chapter discusses the tasks confronting employers in this area and the techniques available for defining age-free job requirements.

WHAT IS NEEDED?

Job requirements should cover both the *what* and the *how* of job performance (H. Levinson, 1976; Oberg, 1972). They need to include a description of the activities that are performed on the job, identifiable or measurable outputs or products that normally result from these activities, and the skills, abilities, and knowledge necessary for successful performance. The idea is to spell out in writing the essential ingredients for effective performance on the job, both as a guideline for selecting the person to fill the job and for guiding (and later evaluating) the performance of the person on the job.

It would seem an easy-enough task to write such a description for a job. In fact, job descriptions already exist in many companies for salary administration purposes. But these documents typically focus on certain job factors such as complexity, scope, number of subordinates, assets controlled, and examples of responsibilities. Job requirements for other personnel purposes need to give greater consideration to the activities required on the job and the specific skills, knowledge, and abilities required. Further, typical job descriptions suffer from subjectivity—they are often prepared by job incumbents or supervisors and then modified and approved by staff personnel and/or a committee charged with administration of the job evaluation and salary administration system.

The task of defining job requirements is difficult because the results must be demonstrably related to the actual jobs. That is, the courts have favored job requirements that are empirically derived—developed through analysis of the actual work performed on each job. It is important to obtain information directly from the source, the person actually doing the work on a job. Work analysis techniques may be applied that minimize subjectivity and help assure a complete and valid definition of a job's content and requirements.

Any work analysis approach has the aim of providing management with an in-depth understanding of the content and requirements of a position. The various techniques available range from broad descriptions of jobs to highly detailed, weighted, task definitions. The degree of detail and the nature of the content (and therefore the techniques applied) vary with the nature of the jobs under study and the purposes of the analysis. Work analysis, variously called job analysis, activity analysis, task analysis, or work study, is the basic methodology by which job requirements are defined empirically.

ACTIVITIES REQUIRED ON THE JOB

The fundamental information used in defining job requirements relates to the activities actually performed. What does a person actually do on the job? What should a person do on the job? How is the job changing or should it be changing? What specific types of activities are to be performed on the job? What proportion of time is to be devoted to each activity? What is the relative importance of each type of activity? These are basic questions to be answered through empirical work analysis.

For salary administration purposes, a job description typically includes a paragraph or two summarizing, in a general way, the nature of the job and the activities performed. This is an excellent starting point for examining the activities required on a job. The description simply needs to be expanded, utilizing information provided by the job incumbent, supervisors, job analysts (observers), and others who know what the job requires.

The result is a listing of activities, preferably grouped into activity groupings (or roles). A framework used for this purpose by several companies includes the following headings for activity groupings:

1 Task Specialist (e.g., performing technical operations, directing technical operations of others, evaluating technical results)

2 Team Member (e.g., team participation, meeting with peers and counterparts, building and maintaining working relationships)

3 Leader (e.g., setting goals for/with others, reviewing performance, instructing and training, organizing, planning)

4 Company Representative (e.g., selling, negotiating, servicing, governmental relations, public relations)

5 Administrator (e.g., budgeting and control, personnel administration, allocating time, setting priorities, resource allocation)

6 Changemaker (Entrepreneur) (e.g., identifying opportunities for change, long-range planning, implementing changes).

As another example, the job of the training and development specialist has been analyzed as comprising 14 primary activity groupings, which represent roles performed; 104 specific activities comprise these roles. The framework is useful for defining the job of a particular trainer, as it facilitates a comprehensive view of the activities that are currently being performed and that could or should be performed as part of the job (Pinto and Walker, 1978).

The matter of actual versus "could or should" is pertinent to the definition of job requirements. It is difficult, of course, to define actual behavior, because even the incumbent's own information is perceptual and subject to distortion. Any data collection procedure involves someone's perceptions of actual behavior. Analyzing work as it should be performed or is planned to be performed in an organization may be a practical approach, but the quality of the necessary subjective judgments is improved by first concentrating on the actual behaviors. Also, from the viewpoint of the courts, *what actually is* is more defensible than notions of *what could or should be* performed on a job (Pinto and Walker, 1978).

WORK OUTPUTS OR STANDARDS

When we consider job requirements we often think of the standards of performance. And it is natural to think of work in terms of the outputs or results attained.

Measures of work outputs are important in designing jobs, determining staffing requirements, setting criteria for employee selection, setting performance standards and objectives, and evaluating job worth for compensation purposes. As a rule, specific work outputs are more easily identified and measured on operative jobs where individual tasks lead to observable results (e.g., the number of coils wound, the number of insurance policies sold, or number of letters typed per day). Here engineering of the work requires a study of the outputs in relation to larger work systems, equipment, flows of work and materials, time and motion patterns, and so forth.

At managerial, professional, and technical levels, however, specific outputs are more difficult to identify, and measures become more subjective. The courts have acknowledged this problem and have agreed that it is necessary on such jobs to identify the goals and circumstances underlying the subjective criteria. Attention thus turns to the efforts expended and the overall results attained by a group or organization rather than individual outputs. To focus on specific outputs becomes entwined with the work of others. Outputs, although appealing because they may be quantitative, are less useful, because qualitative and behavioral factors are more important, at least for the purposes of defining job requirements.

COMPETENCIES

This brings us to the skills, knowledge, and abilities required for performance on a job. Competencies are abilities to perform specified activities. It is, therefore, the flip side of the activities performed and obviously related to the outputs achieved, where applicable. A competency is required on a job, then, when it is necessary to perform certain activities successfully—it is then empirically relevant. And in the view of the courts, it is "valid."

For purposes of appraisal and selection, it is necessary to know what skills, abilities, knowledge, and, possibly, values and attitudes are required to perform a job effectively. In implementing flexible retirement, job competencies are essential for planning job assignments, defining career paths, and modifying work arrangements that may tap individual skills and abilities.

Traditionally, employers have concentrated on obvious factors such as age, length of service, job experience, education, and personal traits. Although these characteristics are discrete and identifiable, they are not necessarily relevant to job requirements. Increasingly, employers are defining competencies in behavioral terms—in ways that allow individuals to know whether they qualify and, if not, whether they wish to develop the necessary skills, abilities, and knowledge. For example, the activity of typing manuscripts may be interpreted as a competency as "ability to type manuscripts." Of course even this is a general competency which involves a number of subcomponents which may be further analyzed as considered necessary and appropriate in a given application.

For nearly 20 years, the U.S. Air Force has maintained descriptions of specializations based on task analysis. One single specialty such as "blood transfusional therapist" may be defined by a ranked list of 1000 task statements. Each statement translates into development-oriented competencies which are used as a basis for planning training programs. The task checklists are updated through empirical studies—surveys of persons on the jobs described.

In many instances age has been applied as a maximum age limit where physical demands or safety are considered job factors. Under a flexible retirement policy, however, age-free standards should be applied. Many employers require annual physical examinations after a certain age, and continued employment in the affected positions is contingent on passing the examination.

A system designed to evaluate employee capacities without age as a factor has been demonstrated as workable in an experiment in Maine. A medical facility in Portland screened more than 2400 job applicants using a system of profiling physical functions of the individuals with demands of jobs. The system, developed and applied at de Haviland Aircraft of Canada, rates individual physical fitness in seven functional areas: general physique, upper extremities, lower extremities, hearing, eyesight, mentality, and personality. The individual ratings (one to seven on each scale) are matched with a parallel job-demands profile. The experiment, administered by the National Council on the Aging, demonstrated that individuals can be employed productively regardless of age if hiring decisions and job placements are based on functional abilities and work requirements.

In defining job requirements, then, it is very useful to profile the levels required on various skills, abilities, and knowledge in the areas determined to be job related. If each major activity is translated into its component competency requirements and each of these is weighted using a scale of importance, a useful profile can be provided as a guide for individual assessment and development. The weights applied must also be defensible in terms of their job-relatedness. It is a final opportunity for subjectivity to enter into job competency requirements.

Finally, it is noteworthy to remind employers that the semantics of job specifications must be watched. The Department of Labor has aggressively (and successfully) pursued companies that refer to age in any way in job advertisements, agency specifications, and supporting job descriptions. Such terms as "recent graduate," "under 40," "boy," "girl," "girl friday," and "young" are suspect and should be avoided. Even the use of terms that limit job opportunities to only part of the protected age group (40–70) is an ADEA violation. This includes such terms as "age over 50," "retired person," "age 40–50," or "supplement your income." Discrimination within the age group is illegal under the ADEA. With this in mind, companies should not identify certain jobs as appropriate for individuals "near retirement," as this would deprive other capable over-40 employees of opportunity.

DATA COLLECTION

Gathering information on job requirements can be done in a number of ways: interviewing the incumbents or their managers, sending out a questionnaire, or directly observing the work performed. No one of these methods alone seems to be the "best" way to find out about jobs: each has advantages and disadvantages (Prien and Ronan, 1971; Wilson, 1974; McCormick, 1976).

Questionnaires allow the collection of a great deal of data from a large number of people. They may simply be a series of questions calling for a narrative response, such as follows:

Outline below the primary parts of your job and indicate the relative proportion of time and importance applicable to each. Use a typical month as a 100% time frame. Time and importance need not correspond.

Outline below the skills, knowledge, abilities, and experience necessary to perform your job effectively. Be as specific as possible and refer back to the activities you outlined above.

What changes have developed in the job during the past year?

What future changes do you anticipate during the year ahead?

Such narrative data are difficult to analyze and unwieldly to update. Yet the method allows the greatest empiricism—all kinds of work aspects can surface.

Questionnaires may be strengthened by structuring them in the form of activity checklists. Lists of likely activities and competencies and outputs may be listed to guide and structure the responses. These may be developed through interviews and examination of related materials such as existing job descriptions, training manuals, job specifications, and organization charts. Obtaining weighted estimates of applicability for each task creates a quantitative data file that is more easily analyzed and updated. The data may also be used to identify job families or clusters and to define possible career progression paths through the organization. Checklists tailored to an organization (even a type of job category) are favored, but published checklists are available to provide the broad dimensions of jobs. Among the published questionnaires widely used are the Position Analysis Questionnaire (PAQ) and the Position Description Questionnaire (PDQ). Many are cropping up in response to the demand for tools in job requirements analysis.

Of course, use of questionnaires can be supplemented with interviews. Traditional job analysis, including the Functional Job Analysis technique adapted for use by the federal government relies on interviews as well as structured data collection. Also, discussions of jobs by groups of knowledgeable persons (managers and staff) can go a long way to provide necessary detail on job content and requirements. A technique called Guidelines-Oriented Job Analysis (GOJA) centers on the generation of task statements and the weighting of them by a panel. Interviews and group sessions are time consuming, and therefore costly, but they add richness to the data obtained. Personal discussion can help clarify what certain activities involve and can place certain requirements in a realistic perspective.

Direct observation of work as it is performed, probably the oldest technique, dating back to time-and-motion studies, is always an appealing alternative technique. The problems persist of assuring a representative sampling of the work and of drawing valid conclusions about the overall job. On managerial, professional, and technical work, observation is fascinating, but largely impractical for the purposes outlined here (Mintzberg, 1973).

END RESULTS

Regardless of the technique used, the process of work analysis should result in a description of what individuals actually do on their jobs, tempered to the extent possible by justifiable company standards of desired performance (what individuals should do). It should also yield a definition of results or outputs normally associated with performance on the position, with measures or indicators provided (and actual standards, where applicable). Third, it should yield a definition of the skills, knowledge areas, abilities (including physical requirements), and related experience or training demonstrated to be relevant to the activities performed.

These results provide an age-free basis for personnel actions, including appraisal, job assignment and transfer, and termination.

CHAPTER NINE

THE DECLINING PERFORMER:
TERMINATE OR TOLERATE

When someone's made his contribution,
you don't just kick him in the rear—A
spokesperson for General Motors at the
House Committee hearings.

Terminating an older worker is a very distasteful task for
any manager. Even if the individual's performance is clearly
deficient, it just does not seem right to end a career unilaterally. In many companies it has always seemed fair to allow
an older employee to stay on until retirement age, even if
capabilities are not quite up to the prevailing standard. And
mandatory retirement policies have supported this philosophy by providing a maximum age ceiling. Those employees
who have not retired early on a voluntary basis are uniformly required to leave at the age of 65.

But now the tenure tradition is repealed, and companies
run the risk of having some employees stay on "indefinitely."
Without mandatory retirement, how can an employer "get
rid" of poor performers without facing charges of age discrimination? How can older employees be forced to retire
without breaking the law or breaking their hearts? These are
difficult questions, ones that concern companies with large
numbers of older workers who may wish to stay on beyond 65.

This chapter examines the scope of this problem and discusses the ways employee terminations can be handled effectively. The focus is on managerial, professional, and technical personnel, because other workers are usually covered by agreements or contracts governing termination procedures.

MANAGERIAL CONCERNS

The principal fear that managers have regarding the end of mandatory retirement is that some of the worst performers simply will not retire voluntarily. With liberalized early retirement programs, the best performers, along with the worst, will leave. This means the companies may find themselves staffed with the dregs of its older work force. And this certainly does not strengthen management desires to offer special retirement inducements or career development assistance to older workers.

"The more we sweeten our early retirement program," notes one personnel manager, "the more likely we are to lose some of our key senior people. They're the ones who have the spunk to go out and find another job, and still take our pension too." Inducements for early retirement may appeal to the superior performers as well as the poorer performers. It is a price to be paid, but it may be a high price.

And then, we still have a few "Old Charlies" hanging around. Without a mandatory retirement age, an employer must tolerate them until they leave voluntarily (or die or become disabled) or terminate them for inadequate performance. That's a tough bullet to bite. By forcing people to retire, employers have not had to face up to performance problems.

The dilemma stems from the problem discussed in previous chapters—assessing individual performance relative to established, objective standards. The unilateral termination of an employee aged 55 or 60 suffers a social stigma of being cruel and unfair, and thus requires an even stronger justification (and objectivity) than might the termination of a younger worker. Older employees often have few career options other than retirement, particularly employees (including some "Old Charlies") who have "given their lives" to the company and are highly loyal to it. To say that they can no longer make an adequate contribution is an onerous judgment by a manager.

A MIXED BAG OF CASES

It is difficult to apply a general rule in terminations because cases vary widely. A simple classification of four types of cases is presented in Figure 1. The key differences identified are based on the performance effectiveness of the employees and their inclination toward retirement versus continued work.

Superior performers may be attracted to second careers in other companies unless sufficiently challenging work opportunities and attractive compensation opportunities are available. Too often, many outstanding professionals and managers retire early and take a new position with another

	Inclined to Retire Early or "On Time"	Inclined to Stay On Working
Superior Performers	Motivate them to stay and work through attractive career opportunities and superior compensation	Utilize their talents well and keep them motivated
Poorer Performers	Induce them to retire through early-retirement programs	Terminate or tolerate

Figure 1. The Mixed Bag of Performers.

company, but taking an enriched early retirement benefit package with them. A company cannot prohibit such "double dipping" or the voluntary separations by superior performers. But it can certainly do whatever it can to make company work and career opportunities attractive. This means specific career guidance and careful job design for high performers, just as are provided for *young* high performers, are desireable. It means that older employees must not be taken for granted.

Of course, special early retirement programs must be available to all employees of a class unless they are unique or informal arrangements. Accordingly, management cannot say who will elect to retire and who will stay. Positive incentives to stay and work for superior performers and disincentives for poorer performers seem to be a logical approach, if not a commonly applied approach. The age act does not ban discrimination on the basis of performance. Nor does it require equal treatment of all older employees in the terms and conditions of employment, as long as age itself is not a factor.

It is legal and feasible, then, to induce poorer performers to retire early. Incentives may include the positive and attractive benefit provisions and supplements. Disincentives may include less attractive job assignments, exclusion from communications, exclusion from career development and professional activities, and the like. The positive incentives are, of course, preferable and have worked effectively among employees who have an inclination to retire anyway.

For the superior performers who have an inclination to stay on rather than retire, the employer should strive to utilize effectively the talents offered and to keep the individuals motivated through their work. These, of course, are rare individuals, often of an entrepreneurial character. By and large, they have not represented a significant management problem because of their small number and their evident ability to make a contribution.

The final group is the focus of this chapter: the poorer performers who have an inclination to stay. If they are "forced to retire" without an adequate performance-based justification, they have grounds for filing an age discrimination charge. More importantly, they are the toughest group to confront and to help come to grips with their own aging and career patterns. Although they may represent fewer than one in ten employees over the age of 60, they pose a difficult responsibility for management.

Management bears an ethical, legal, and administrative responsibility to terminate employees, including older employees, who demonstrate ineffective performance. It is unfair to other workers, to stockholders, and to customers to allow "deadwood" to burden an organization. These are harsh terms, but ones that many companies hold to be important. Hence in the Senate hearings the outcry of employers was that "banning mandatory retirement deprives management of a useful tool in the orderly separation of older employees from the work force."

CRITERIA FOR TERMINATIONS

The primary criterion acceptable as a basis for termination is performance. Performance standards (or job requirements) are therefore required, and objective judgments or evidence of individual performance relative to these standards are also required. Additionally, affected employees should know what their appraisers think of their performance and should be given the chance to improve. The need for warnings of poor (unacceptable) performance has been demonstrated in recent court cases.

If job performance falls below a minimally acceptable standard (which has been uniformly applied without regard to age), the performance evaluations and the standards themselves are the criteria for termination actions. Both need to be well defined and documented. But many older employees falter on a job because of declining physical abilities. Here an employer may be obliged to find alternate work suited to the individual's capabilities that does not require the specific impaired capacities. The rules governing affirmative action programs for the handicapped are not clearly defined as they apply to aging. Certainly, failing eyesight, hearing, dexterity, agility, and other capacities represent disabling conditions for work.

Other limitations, such as obsolescence of skills and knowledge or inability to master a new job assignment or a restructured job assignment, may be overcome by alternative work arrangements. Older employees may be retrained or reassigned to work that better utilizes their level of capabilities. The various tools of flexible retirement practice may be introduced instead of outright termination for ineffective performance.

The ADEA does not require affirmative action on behalf of older employees. Neither does it specifically require an employer to find work that can match an individual's changing capacities. As a responsible employer, however, poor performance on a particular job may not be an adequate basis for termination. And the relentless trend toward consideration of employee rights may ultimately lead to requirements that employers retain and utilize older workers, even poor performers and "disabled" individuals.

It is also appropriate for an employer to consider whether an individual is truly "dispensible." It is often an older employee who seems to know how to make an operation tick.

- Does the individual have specific or unique expertise or knowledge that is not present elsewhere in the organization or that is difficult to recruit/develop?

- Is the experience of the individual so unusual or diverse that it would be difficult to replace (by younger, less experienced talent)?

- Does the individual rank well when compared to others in terms of usable skills, knowledge, or experience (regardless of current job assignment)?

- Is there age bias in the appraisals of the individual's performance? In the opportunity for the individual to perform effectively due to age bias on the job?

- Are there extraordinary circumstances that may account for a temporary period of poor performance (e.g., death of spouse)?

If responses are affirmative to such questions, perhaps termination is not appropriate. Alternatives should be considered to prevent the loss of the individual to the organization.

EXPLAINING WHY

The criteria applied in a termination need to be specified, documented, and explained to those affected. And the individual employee is not alone. A termination has important effects on the "survivors"—the other employees who continue working. These other workers learn from terminations and thereby formulate judgments of management practices. Implicit in their learning is their own fear of possible similar treatment someday.

The criteria typically communicated to employees being terminated (terminees, dismissees) are generalities. The reasons for dismissal are usually vague, arbitrary, and inconsistent. The manager is in an uncomfortable position and would prefer to avoid getting into negative details—and particularly avoid any confrontation with the employee regarding the criteria or the validity of the evidence. Criteria, then, are not often discussed except in general terms (e.g., "We really like you but we don't really need you.").

A related problem is reliance on external factors as the stated reason for terminations: elimination of work, cost-reduction necessities, lessened market demand, loss of vital projects or customers, or "the system made me do it." Peter Drucker once observed that it is easier for managers to say "yes" frequently regarding staffing matters and then say "no" all at once when the economy is conveniently in a downturn. In this way, age discrimination can be conveniently cloaked in a rationale of economic necessity.

Employees not directly affected by terminations are indirectly affected. Although there may be a positive effect in some organizations by clearing out "deadwood" and showing management's ability (and willingness) to take tough personnel actions, there may be negative effects as well. The criteria applied in terminations typically are mysterious. Secrecy clouds the reasons for terminations, and rumors often emerge to explain such personnel actions. Sometimes reasons are soon forgotten, just as the departed employees are forgotten; in other instances history is rewritten by new rumors and rationalizations for terminations. Simply, a lack of clearly specified criteria for terminations creates a degree of confusion, uncertainty, and anxiety among employees remaining in an organization.

Increasingly, companies are reluctant to disclose reasons for terminations that may suggest age discrimination. It is no longer okay to say that terminations are intended to bring "younger blood" into management or to strengthen the company's competitiveness. Even subtle age discrimination, as appeared in the Sandia Laboratories case in which a reduction in force based on performance adversely affected older scientists and engineers, is being carefully avoided. It is not likely that a company will announce to the world that it needs or prefers younger talent, as IBM did when it introduced a mandatory retirement age of 60 for its executives. IBM cited the need for young, aggressive talent to meet the demands of a highly competitive industry. Under the ADEA, terminations must be related to job performance.

HOW TO TERMINATE AN OLDER EMPLOYEE

The toughest aspect of terminating an employee is the actual act of confrontation. Nobody enjoys telling an older employee his career is over, whatever the reason. Because the task is so distasteful and difficult, it is often poorly done, resulting in ill feelings, doubts, and sometimes litigation. To an extent, the manner in which management handles terminations is a measure of its effectiveness in dealing with sensitive issues. In fact, the task is so much an indicator of the interpersonal effectiveness of managers that incidents may be generalized by employees and other observers as representative of the company's management style.

Of course, alternatives to terminations should be explored fully before an action is taken. As discussed above, an employee may be suited for other positions or may be induced to retire voluntarily. From a legal standpoint, it would be a good idea to document the alternatives considered, the assistance provided to the employees, and the outcomes of such efforts. Many companies hold that after 30 years' service, an employee deserves a sincere effort by the company to minimize negative or abrupt actions. The long-service employee deserves extenuating consideration by a company.

Accordingly, the employee should know of management's dissatisfaction with performance and know what courses of action are being considered. Ideally, the employee participates in the deliberation process, considering what could be done to improve performance, modify the work demands, change job assignments, and so forth. Such patent facts as poor attendance, tardiness, insubordination, and appraisal results should be recorded and, ideally, discussed with the employee.

Typically there is a barrier to terminations in an organization: there are no rewards to managers for taking such actions. In fact, managers who terminate employees (particularly older, long-service employees) may become reputed to be "axemen." Hence, as in the federal civil service, few managers are willing to bite the bullet and terminate anyone, regardless of the justification. Inaction is easier to justify and bears far less risk of reprisal. And inaction can be blamed on bureaucratic constraints on terminations, EEO and age discrimination constraints, or personnel regulations. Thus to encourage managers to take actions, companies need to clear procedural obstacles and give positive recognition to those who exercise terminations effectively. Terminations need to be regarded as an important part of a manager's job rather than a risky, no-win task to be avoided at all costs.

Managers need to be encouraged also to confront employees regarding unsatisfactory performance and discuss the possibility of termination. Too often they let the problem get worse, or *make* it worse by grating the employee. "We don't fire people; they fire themselves." Poorer performers are often pushed aside into make-work jobs and ignored, with the assumption that they will either stay out of the way or will quit/retire voluntarily. In other cases, managers chafe employees by giving them undesirable assignments, harassing them regarding details and procedures, and generally minimizing positive reinforcements. Yet discouraging employees into quitting or retiring may be considered by some observers to be unfair or poor management practice. Rather, managers should be directed and trained to face up to each individual employee's performance and act on individual career plans that suit the employee's abilities, performance, and the company's needs.

Finally, when the act of termination is taken, managers should spell out the reasons and review the steps leading up to this final action. Some employers have adopted a policy forbidding discussion of reasons for terminations, based on the assumption that information provided may later appear as evidence in litigation. But if properly equipped and prepared, managers can conduct a termination in a way that serves both the individual's and the company's needs. There is no place today for the managerial view that reasons for terminating are the "company's business." Similarly, unfounded "song-and-dance" rationalizations contrived to make the terminee feel "better" are inappropriate. Honesty is the best policy for all parties concerned.

HANDLING THE TERMINATION INTERVIEW

Who should handle terminations? The answer has varied, and there is no simple answer. Some feel it is the responsibility of the immediate supervisor; others feel that the personnel department should be involved. For lower-level employees, the matter is usually handled either by the personnel department or by managers higher than the immediate supervisor. For managerial, professional, and technical employees, the personnel department is not always well acquainted with the specific aspects of the situation or the job. Accordingly, terminations are handled by the managers in the local organizational unit.

When should terminated employees be required to leave? This question, too, has been answered many ways. For executives, up to a year has often been allowed to ease the departure. Commonly, though, companies require (or at least allow) terminated employees to leave immediately. For older, long-service employees, immediate departure is not essential. Risks of theft, damage, or disruptions are unlikely. And if the individual reacts positively, perhaps taking a view that the departure is voluntary, he may wish to stay and ease the transition for a successor. Again, there is no simple answer; each case has different circumstances that dictate the most effective timing.

A termination interview should be conducted in a private office under conditions that allow a full and frank discussion of the situation. No longer is the Friday afternoon termination the accepted practice. ("Take the rest of the afternoon to clean out your desk—You're fired.") To minimize negative feelings and the possibility of litigation, an interview needs to be thorough and discussive. The following points are important:

- Minimize uncertainty, speculation, and rumor by spelling out the actual facts and circumstances leading to the action.

- Review alternative options that are open or that have been considered, including voluntary early retirement.

- Allow the individual to ask questions and make observations pertinent to the case.

- Focus on the future of the individual and provide constructive help and guidance; don't dwell on the past.

- Develop the facts and alternatives in a step-by-step and logical manner; don't be abrupt and terse.

- Review written documentation pertaining to performance-based termination criteria.

- Offer counseling on outplacement services, severance pay and benefits, and other assistance that are available to the employee.

- Explain the company policy regarding rehiring and the employee's rights and likely evaluation should he apply for a position.

- Explain the reasons the company will give to companies checking employment references and to other employees.

- Seek the employee's reactions and feelings regarding performance, career, and leaving (typical exit-interview topics).

The older employee is less likely to be concerned with future employment and less likely to be hostile toward management.

Often a termination is an expected outcome that the individual simply did not want to initiate. And the future likely holds retirement and an adjustment to retirement. The most common reaction to terminations (or forced retirements) is concern with the fairness of treatment. The above guidelines ameliorate the negative effects of terminations of older employees and bring objectivity and interpersonal discussion to the forefront. This maximizes fairness of treatment.

AGING AND RETIREMENT

CHAPTER TEN

HOW EMPLOYEES DECIDE WHEN TO RETIRE

Like most people, I never gave much thought to retirement when I was younger. I just assumed that all people over sixty-five were eager to retire and wanted nothing more than the right to go fishing 365 days a year—Paul Woodring, "Why Sixty-Five," *Saturday Review* (August 7, 1976).

The decision faced by employees is not *whether* to retire, but *when* to retire. The decision to retire is one of timing. And the timing is a matter of personal, voluntary choice (at least until the age of 70 under the ADEA). With recent liberalization of early retirement provisions in many companies, the decision to retire has already become largely a voluntary one. Most employees have, in fact, set their own retirement dates, with weight given their personal health, feelings, finances, and interests.

With the likely possibility of no mandatory retirement age in many companies, an understanding is needed of the factors influencing the decision to retire. Many company spokesmen in the Congressional hearings voiced fears that without an age ceiling for employment, a flood of employees would continue working. A study by Sears, Roebuck suggested that "as many as one-third" of the firm's retirees might continue to work under the new rules. To allay management concerns and to manage effectively the flow of workers over the age-65 "watershed" (whether it is a flood or a trickle), managers need to consider how employees decide to retire.

This chapter provides a perspective of the retirement decision and its impact on employers and our society. A model is proposed that identifies the determinants of individual retirement timing, and several of the most important determinants are discussed. Subsequent chapters discuss pertinent biological and psychological facts of aging and patterns of postretirement activities and attitudes regarding retirement and aging. Together, these chapters provide a glimpse of the field of gerontology—the field of study devoted to aging, work, and retirement.

A RETIREMENT PERSPECTIVE

Is retirement "the golden years," or is it "the human scrap heap"? In reality it may be either, depending on a multitude of factors interrelated in a complex process. Retirement is a paradox in our society. On one hand, retirement is viewed as a reward for a lifetime of productive work. It is a highly regarded period for full-time leisure activities. On the other hand, the work ethic continues to be strong in our society, making the transition from work to full-time leisure extremely difficult for some. Work and the fruits of labor are viewed as good; laziness, handouts, and welfare are viewed as bad. Thus individuals about to retire from 40 or more years of work may experience a tremendous shock in the transition from being a producing member of society to drawing an income "for doing nothing" in retirement.

Other factors are creating social changes which are mirrored in American institutions. The composition of the population is altering in terms of age and income distribution, and the values of a youth-oriented society are increasingly being felt. Early retirement is becoming a specific objective of many young people (of course, many think of the age of 35 as old). Retirement is increasingly acceptable to older workers. Society is more affluent, and more and more emphasis is placed on leisure-time activities. The government, through Social Security and Medicare programs, is reducing the financial uncertainties of retirement in response to the needs of the portion of the population that is of retirement age. At the same time company policies and benefits for early retirement have become more liberal. Although this is partly due to the drive of the unions, the effects are apparent at all levels. Top executives commonly leave to take on new projects; professionals opt out to pursue personal interests.

Existing research literature does not provide systematic attention to "why or how people retire" in this changing context. We have a rather fragmentary view of retirement and the dynamics among the many factors that affect individual retirement decisions, governmental policy and planning decisions, and management decisions about what kinds of retirement options to offer. A cohesive approach for understanding the retirement process is needed if we are to improve the impact of retirement on the individual, on the organization, and on our society.

HOW THE RETIREMENT DECISION FITS IN

On the premise that retirement is a natural step in an individual's career, the focal point of a retirement model is the retirement decision: "At what age should I retire?" The decision is described in terms of age, but is not necessarily determined by age. The decision to retire may also be influenced by a number of variables, outlined below. When retirement is mandatory, institutional variables are dominant. As retirement becomes more voluntary, individual and societal variables play a greater role. As illustrated in Figure 1, the retirement decision has three primary areas of impact: on individual satisfaction in retirement, on organizations (in terms of both costs and benefits), and on our social system (Walker and Price, 1976; Walker and Price, 1974).

The primary variables influencing the decision to retire are as follows:

Environmental Variables

Demographics: The age, income, and sex characteristics of the population. For example, older workers with adequate wealth and retirement benefits may be more likely to retire than older workers in a poorer society, where retirement might mean starvation.

Environment: The state of the economy, the type of business or industry, the level of technology are all factors. During periods of inflation, for example, workers may be reluctant to retire and be dependent upon a fixed income which would rapidly lose its purchasing power. If technological change is rapid, employees may opt to retire rather than be constantly reeducated.

Governmental Policies and Programs: Policies that may foster earlier retirement include tax advantages for retired persons, special programs for the aged, comprehensive medical care, and Social Security benefits linked to the cost of living.

Culture Values: A high value on work may tend to discourage individuals from retiring; high value on leisure encourages retirement. Socially determined values influence attitudes toward retirement and "proper" retirement timing.

Organizational Variables

Policies and Values: How the organization views retirement and its older employees may affect individual retirement decisions.

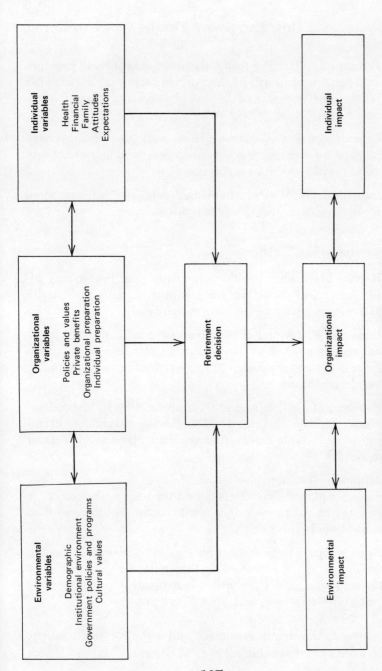

Figure 1. Retirement: A Systems Perspective.

Private Benefits: For many, the retirement income from private pension plans will be their primary source of income after retirement. The design of the plan plays a major role in the economic feasibility of retiring early.

Organizational Preparation: How well the company has planned for the succession of employees who may retire may affect decisions to retire or stay on.

Individual Preparation: Individuals who are better prepared for retirement are more likely to retire early.

Individual Variables

Health: Individual health, particularly poor health, may affect retirement timing. Individuals often indicate poor health as a primary reason for deciding to retire early.

Financial Factors: Personal financial conditions, both present and anticipated, may be a crucial factor. If a person thinks there is not enough money to live on in retirement, the timing may be postponed.

Family: Marital status and the responsibility for dependents also affects the retirement decision. Having two children in college would tend to defer retirement timing because of financial demands.

Attitudes: Feelings about work, leisure, retirement, the job, and one's place in life, all may affect the retirement decision. A person who enjoys working is less likely to want to retire than a dissatisfied worker.

Expectations: Individuals who expect retirement to be the "golden years" may be more likely to retire early and to accept the transition more readily than individuals who feel they are being rejected at work and "forced" to leave.

These variables are interrelated, and some are more salient than others in influencing retirement decisions.

THE RETIREMENT DECISION

If individuals are forced to retire at some age (e.g., 70), the decision to retire is at least partially out of their control. They cannot stay beyond a mandatory retirement age, but they still might be able to choose to retire prior to that age if they are willing to accept the retirement income benefits provided. Thus even if there is a mandatory retirement age in an organization, there still remains an opportunity for individual retirement decision making. If there is flexible retirement, the individual dominates the retirement timing decision.

Age itself, research and advocacy suggest, should not be the determinant of retirement decisions; rather, it is a descriptor of the result—retirement timing in the chronological life of the individual. Individual capabilities, attitudes, and health are determinants—and they are not strictly functions of age. Some individuals at the age of 80 may be less ready for retirement than others at the age of 50. Hence there is an attractive logical argument for greater flexibility in retirement timing.

Yet the analysis of the decision to retire is the question of *when* to retire, and that is normally specified in terms of age. Until relatively recently, retirement age has been set largely by the employer: Employees retired when and only when the employer decided that they should retire, however arbitrary the age selected might be.

With the end of mandatory retirement, employees may now decide to retire when they feel that the timing is personally "right." Throughout this book we have used the term "early retirement" as a phrase meaning retirement timing sometime before the norm and certainly at an age below the ceiling of age 70 represented in the ADEA, as amended. But, as a result of individual volition in retirement decision making, the term "early" is somewhat misleading, for what is early for one person may be just right for another. In short, there is nothing "early" about early retirement except the age of a retiree relative to ages of other retirees. And if chronological age is not indicative of capacities and interests, then "early" retirement timing is not a very meaningful notion.

As noted, the focus of management attention should be on the factors that affect the individual's decision to retire, and not on age as a determinant of retirement timing. The factors logically flow from the list previously given. As shown in Figure 2, some factors tend to accelerate retirement timing; others tend to delay retirement. This concept is useful to managers in considering both individual employee retirement decisions and broader trends in retirement timing.

Figure 2. Factors Affecting the Retirement Decision.

HEALTH

A healthy individual is more likely to remain on the job than an individual who is experiencing health problems. Yet health is a relative condition, influenced by individual perceptions and comparisons with the health of others. Studies have shown that after retirement individual perceptions of health tend to improve, in part because of the new comparison basis (See Chapter 11).

Conversely, poor health is often cited as a reason for retirement, particularly early retirement. In fact, it is a primary reason for voluntary retirements (Kimmel, Price, and Walker, 1978). Many individuals retire because of disabilities; others may cite health because it is a socially acceptable reason for retiring (Pollman, 1971; Orbach, 1969).

A Social Security study published in 1971 indicated that health was the most important reason cited for retirement. Of workers who retire before the age of 65, the responses of 54% indicated poor health as the reason. Poor health included all identifiable physical problems or an inability to keep up with the pace of work. At 65, the number of workers who left their jobs primarily because of health dropped to less than 25%—clearly reflecting the importance of health in the early retirement decision. It should be noted that the study centered on men rather than all Social Security retirees (Smedley, 1974).

FEELINGS ABOUT RETIREMENT

The second-largest category in the Social Security study was those who indicated they retired early because they wanted to. Their responses ranged from mildly negative toward work to a positive anticipation of retirement. This finding is supported by other studies indicating that, after health, feelings about retirement are the most important consideration (Kimmel, Price, and Walker, 1978).

As retirement develops a positive image, people do not feel uncertain or guilty about retiring (Orbach, 1969). Retirement is becoming more of an anticipated feature of the life cycle; it is seen as normal and good. It is not seen as a disruption of one's life, as it has in the past. And this is important, given the increased life expectancy at retirement age.

For some individuals, retirement from one career or organization is a step toward another. Second careers are undertaken primarily to supplement retirement income, but often also to remain active. Research also suggests that postretirement employment is inversely related to educational level of retirees (Owen, 1967). Individuals with lower levels of education usually have had lower-level, lower-paying jobs when working and are more likely to find similar work after retirement. Of course, they are more likely to need supplemental retirement income as well. Second careers are quite common for retired military officers, who can retire with as little as 20 years of service.

A 1978 survey by the Conference Board examined postretirement activities of middle- and top-level managers in United States firms. Two-thirds of the 3800 respondents have been engaged in postretirement work, paid or unpaid. It was found that most individuals undertook work, paid or volunteer, in areas similar to their earlier careers. However, many have undertaken work in entirely different occupations (Wikstrom, 1978).

Job dissatisfaction also affects the retirement decision. Lower-level workers particularly retire voluntarily (and early) to get away from the job (Barfield and Morgan, 1969). Higher-level employees (managers and professionals) are more likely to retire to get to retirement, and not so much because of negative job feelings.

Many employees retire early because of increased pressures felt in their job and their career. Rather than seek retraining for another job or wait to get fired, they opt for retirement. The pressures of rapid technological and organizational changes often make older employees feel uneasy about their staying on. Rather than continuing to feel strained and uncomfortable in their changing work environment they retire voluntarily. In our youth-oriented society there is also a felt pressure for older workers to make room for younger workers. Barfield and Morgan report that 62% of their respondents (auto workers) believed that young people thought that older people should retire early (Barfield and Morgan, 1969).

Many employees have retired voluntarily to avoid unpleasant confrontations with their managers regarding unsatisfactory performance. When employees "get the message" that performance is unacceptable, they often voluntarily decide to retire (usually early) rather than lose face through performance discussions and possible termination proceedings. It is important, therefore, for management to wield the performance appraisal process with vigor, so that these decisions to retire will continue to be made voluntarily. Ideally, no older employee should be unilaterally terminated; each employee should have the sense to retire when best for all concerned.

Other associated factors tend to push retirement timing up. Some people feel that retirement removes them from the satisfactions of their job and social relationships with coworkers. Thus retirement reduces overall life satisfaction. One study reported that 37% of the men and 25% of the women felt that their satisfaction with life would be lowered by retirement (Streib and Schneider, 1971). Related to this is a fear of aging and death. Feelings that retirement indicates old age are common, and old age means impending death. By postponing retirement, the individual feels he is avoiding old age.

There are also some employees who feel strongly that

working is what life is all about. The work ethic is sometimes so strong that employees are not easily persuaded to retire at all. The concept of full-time leisure is alien and distasteful. Even among retirees who feel they have adequate financial resources, some resent the transition because they feel that working for pay is highly important.

Companies, too, sometimes press to defer retirements of some individuals. Retirement removes talent from a company—talent that may be vital to effective operations (Walker and Price, 1974). In this context more flexible retirement may work to the advantage of companies who have highly competent older employees in certain key positions (e.g., operations superintendents, technical positions, research scientists, salespersons).

INCOME AND FINANCIAL CONDITION

Money is often thought of as a key factor in the decision to retire: "Can I afford to retire now?" Retirement income is constrained by inflation, as projected purchasing power may diminish in a very few years.

Pension benefits, deferred profit sharing, savings, annuities, Social Security benefits, and other income sources all combine to provide the income needed for retirement. A notion has long been proposed that retirement income comprises a three-legged stool: employer-provided benefits, public benefits, and personal savings. Employees who have a projected adequate income flow from these three areas are likely to retire voluntarily and early. Studies of early retirement indicate that income is often considered the most important variable in the decision to retire.

"Workers will retire—if they can afford to," agrees Northwestern University Professor Frank Cassell. "Unfortunately, inflation is rapidly eroding all pensions, and cost-of-living clauses for pensions are too costly for most firms to even consider" (Nekvasil, 1978). Total income is often less important than the insurance and other benefits. Insecurity in retirement stems not only from a fear of not having enough money to live on a day-to-day basis; it also comes from the fear that costly illnesses will occur. Hence early retirement is attractive to those like the auto workers, who have liberal postretirement benefits plus cost-of-living adjustments. Higher-level executives and professionals are inclined to retire early because they can afford to and can look forward to leisure activities or second careers. The middle group, salaried employees who are not represented by UAW-type plans, face greater uncertainties relating to benefits and inflation. Economic necessity, therefore, dictates that they defer retirement until they "have to" or until they feel income provisions are adequate.

SUMMARY

In summary, there is no simple answer to the questions, "When will people retire if they have a flexible retirement policy?" and "How do employees go about deciding when they will retire?" But research and experience indicate that certain factors are important, and the combination of these factors varies with the individuals facing the retirement decision.

Research suggests that health is an important factor, as are income and finances. But feelings about retirement, a complex area involving numerous variables, also are important determinants and are subject to management influence. The following chapters examine in further detail the subjects of physical aging and psychological aspects of retirement and aging.

CHAPTER ELEVEN

THE BIOLOGICAL FACTS
OF AGING

Of those over sixty-five, 86% are afflicted with one or more of the chronic degenerative diseases. But few observers emphasize the reverse side of these statistics: 14% do not have these diseases. Though all old people eventually fall prey to deteriorative changes, many seem to escape the major ravages of aging until they are very old indeed—Albert Rosenfeld, *Prolongevity*.

Today there are nearly 22 million Americans 65 and older, nearly seven times the number there were in 1900. Each day about 4000 persons turn 65 and 3000 aged 65 or over die. Because of the net increase in numbers and longevity, we may expect one out of every five Americans to be over 65 by the year 2000.

The growing number of older persons in our society is due in large part to improved physical health. The average human life expectancy has extended from about 22 years of age in the time of ancient Greece to about 71 today. At the turn of the century the life expectancy was 47. Yet even today few live to be 100 years old (only about 13,000 Americans are 100 or older today). Thus the total life *span* has not increased. More people reach age 65, but they then do not live much longer than did their ancestors who reached that age in 1900.

With improved life expectancy and earlier retirements, our society has a much larger older population, and there are many more older people who wish to continue working and are able to work. Yet individual capabilities do diminish with age, and thus managers need to understand what happens to people as they grow older. Myths of aging—older people are rigid, inflexible, feebleminded, forgetful, weak, senile, and boring—need to be reexamined. Physical (biological and intellectual) characteristics of aging need to be recognized and taken into consideration in making individual competency assessments. Psychological characteristics of aging, closely related to retirement and work attitudes of older individuals, need to be recognized and taken into consideration in the management of older workers and the guidance of their careers.

This chapter briefly surveys our knowledge of the physical aspects of aging, drawn from fields of geriatrics (the medical field of study of the aged and their diseases) and gerontology (the interdisciplinary study of the aging process itself). The succeeding chapter surveys what we know about the psychological aspects of aging.

GETTING OLD

The stereotype of older Americans depicts them as being feeble and sick. It is true that older persons commonly suffer from chronic diseases and that basic bodily changes affect physical and mental capacities. But these conditions vary widely among individuals. Only 5% of persons over 65 live in nursing homes or other institutions; only 20% suffer a limitation on mobility or have been hospitalized during the past year. The worst image of an older person as frail and sick may be characteristic of some, but it certainly is not an accurate generalization.

Yet older persons do suffer increasing incapacities. Physiological changes occur, although gradually, throughout adult life. Individuals age at different rates and in different ways. In a sense, older people are less alike than they have ever been, as their numbers grow and diversity increases. Certain patterns of aging may be described, but only on the average.

As individuals grow older, they tend to lose stature. Spinal vertebrae move closer together and muscular weakness contributes to stooping. Of course, older persons sometimes seem shorter simply because younger persons are increasingly taller. Also, with increasing age, bones become lighter and more brittle, partly because of calcium metabolism. The risk of bone breakage, therefore, increases.

Both muscle size and strength diminish with age. But this process actually begins after a peak between 20 and 30 years of age. Although new muscle is regenerated, muscle mass does decrease, because of lessened activity and changes in circulatory and connective tissues. Loss of muscle tissue is particularly noticeable in the small muscles of the hands. Strength of fingers and arms actually reaches maximum levels at about the age of 20 and is sustained until about the age of 40. Leg and trunk muscles peak at 30 and decline thereafter. However, overall muscular strength does not necessarily decrease significantly, because it is also dependent on perceptual and motor capacity (Woodruff and Birren, 1975; Laufer and Fowler, 1971).

With aging there also tends to be a slowing down of reaction time and performance in work. But being slower does not mean being incapacitated. Movement and reaction time tend to be fastest for persons in their early 20s. Consistency of reactions is greatest around the age of 30. Among older persons, however, differences are great and relate in part to the nature and level of activity performed earlier in life. Tasks that were performed frequently may be performed more speedily in older age; performance of tasks may become more difficult, depending on whether they are complex or simple (but complex ones may be performed more easily by some older persons!) (Laufer and Fowler, 1971).

A significant change occurs in the circulation system. The heart and blood vessels become less elastic. The heart rate does not respond as well to stress, the muscles do not contract and relax as fast as they used to, and the arteries tend to resist the flow of blood. After the age of 50, the output of blood from the heart declines by 1% each year. As a result of these changes, heart rate and blood pressure rise and contribute to heart disease and shortness of breath (Anderson, 1978).

An apparent change with aging is increased paleness of skin, along with change in texture, dryness, rigidity, and spots. These changes are a result of increased collagen, a stiff fibrous protein that also contributes to circulatory and muscular problems. Such changes affect the ability of the body to heal wounds and to support the body mechanically. Of course, such changes also affect a person's physical appearance and thus one's self-image, concept, and feelings (Kimmel, 1974).

SENSORY AND MENTAL CAPACITIES

With aging there is a decrease in efficient function in all the senses. Taste, smell, and sense of pain diminish with age, but they do not have a significant effect on capacities (other than loss of appetite and thus nutritional effects). Hearing and vision also diminish, but these are not necessarily serious impairments. Visual acuity (ability to see clearly at a distance), adaptation to darkness, and accommodation (ability of the eye lens to focus on objectives close by) all diminish with age. About 92% of persons 65 and over wear eyeglasses to adjust for failing eyesight. Similarly, the threshold for hearing declines with age, but only 5% of older people use hearing aids. The ability to understand speech and to hear high-pitch sounds also may decrease and have an effect on ability to work (Kimmel, 1974). In most jobs today, however, the sensory demands are well below the capacities of most older workers. This means that these physical changes are often overrated in our impressions of what older people can and cannot do.

Intelligence does not slide downhill from adulthood through old age. Memory, particularly recent memory, does decline, as do cognitive abilities, problem-solving abilities, and creativity. However, verbal skills (e.g., vocabulary), retention of knowledge, and ability to apply education and experience do not tend to decline. Much of the apparent decline in intelligence, as reflected in test scores, is probably due to slower reaction time and slower performance. It is quite possible that commonly used intelligence tests are biased toward younger subjects because of the format and language used (Baltes and Schaie, 1974).

Similarly, learning abilities are not necessarily impaired with advancing age. The slowing of performance with age simply requires a modified approach to training and education for older persons. More selective presentation of materials, a slower rate of pacing to allow full comprehension, more direct relevance of instruction to tasks, and learning by activity methods rather than by memory or abstraction are suggested ways of sustaining learning capacities of older individuals (McFarland, 1976).

Individual creativity and problem-solving capacities are likely to diminish with old age because of reduced cognitive capacities and memory. Redundancy, difficulty in handling new concepts, and inability to make use of efficient strategies in solving problems have been found to be characteristic with aging. Similarly, "rigidity" and "cautiousness" (or avoidance of risk) may be related to reduced abilities to obtain and process information. Yet older people often compensate for reduced abilities by applying judgment, experience and knowledge, and patient (slower) attention to the tasks. In considering the many artists, scholars, scientists, and statesmen who have performed extraordinarily after age 65 or 70, it is difficult to conclude that such intellectual capacities are automatically limited with advancing age.

CHRONIC DISEASES

Aging is not a disease, nor does it imply failing health. Rather, aging is ". . . a decline in physiologic competence that inevitably increases the incidence and intensifies the effects of accidents, disease, and other forms of environmental stress" (Timiras, 1972). Older persons are more susceptible to illness; in fact, chronic conditions represent the number-one health care problem of the older population. Although younger age groups suffer from chronic diseases, the incidence is highest after the age of 65 (86% as opposed to 72% for the age 45–64 age group). Also, many older persons suffer from multiple conditions.

Chronic conditions include such illnesses as heart and circulatory disorders, arthritis and rheumatic diseases, diabetes, cancer, neurological disorders, blindness and deafness, mental retardation, and long-term mental illness. The five most prevalent of these conditions are:

1 Arthritis (38%)
2 Hearing impairments (29%)
3 Vision impairments (20%)
4 Hypertension (20%)
5 Heart conditions (20%)

Females tend to display higher rates of arthritis and hypertension, higher rates of visual disorders, and lower rates of hearing impairments. Prevalence of heart conditions is similar in both sexes. All the chronic diseases except ulcers tend to be more prevalent among the poor (Harris, 1978; Kimmel, 1974).

Though the older population has higher rates of chronic conditions than the younger population, it has relatively lower rates of temporary illnesses (acute conditions). Such medical advances as vaccines, antibiotics, and improved health conditions have primarily benefitted those afflicted with acute diseases, primarily younger people. Hence the sharp increase in life expectancy at birth, but little change at older ages (Kimmel, 1974).

HEALTH

In spite of the prevalence of health problems occurring among older people, most individuals over 65 do not think of themselves as constrained in their day-to-day activities. Although four people in five suffer from at least one health condition, fewer than one in five consider themselves sufficiently handicapped to warrant reduced daily activities. Respondents in a national health survey among the older population asked how they rated their health: 68% indicated "good" or "excellent" (Harris, 1978).

There also appear to be necessary distinctions within the "older population." At a minimum it is appropriate to distinguish the "elderly" (so-called "old old") from the group. The elderly are those persons, typically age 75 and over, who suffer from chronic conditions, are relatively inactive, and are either institutionalized or under close supervisory care. The "young old," on the other hand, are in better health, are more active, and are continuing to act independently. With the expansion of the 65-and-over population, the younger group is obviously increasing at a faster rate than the elderly.

Hence the issues of unfair stereotypes, employment constraints, legal rights, and retirement life styles have emerged as important.

THE LENGTH OF LIFE

As the older population grows larger, it is natural to wonder whether everyone will be living longer. Preservation of life has always been an important priority. Considerable research to extend life expectancy (and the overall life span of man) has been conducted by researchers in the various biological (and chemical) fields (Sheppard, 1977; Rosenfeld, 1976).

Clearly, heredity is a key component involved in the length of life. Already, man's life span is longer than would be expected for a mammal of his size and is the longest-lived species of mammal (Kimmel, 1974). The relatively large size of man's brain may be an important biological factor, as may man's demonstrated capacity to cope with environmental factors. At any rate, genetic or hereditary factors have evolved over countless generations, setting time clocks that are difficult to reset through mere medical advances and hygiene.

One theory of aging holds that the "clock of aging" is built into each cell in the body. Each of the many trillions of cells in the body are controlled by chromosomes. Chromosomes are composed of DNA molecules, whose structures are chemically coded with the body's entire potential hereditary future. Some researchers believe that understanding and controlling DNA may be the key to controlling longevity in man (Rosenfeld, 1976).

Other theories and research efforts focus on related processes of hormone flows, protein synthesis, cellular "waste disposal" (effects of a fatty substance called lipofuscin that relates to aging), immunities, and homeostatic balance/imbalance. Perhaps the most common-sense theory is that the body simply wears out from usage, as does a machine. But, then, the controls of cell maintenance and regeneration lie in DNA. In an interview, gerontologist Alex Comfort observed to Rosenfeld, "The hell of it is that you can seize upon almost any given feature of aging and invent a theory based on it. From one single aspect, it seems that you can usually derive most of the others" (Rosenfeld, 1976, p. 31).

If the fundamental limits on the span of life can be pushed out through biomedical advances, it is possible that we will have a whole new definition of "old." Under favorable conditions, if they are discovered, a person could perhaps live indefinitely.

ENVIRONMENTAL FACTORS IN AGING

Dying of natural causes means that a person "wears out" through cellular aging, without intervention by illness, accident, or disease. Aging is a function of everything that has gone on in a person's life—heredity, activity, nutrition, exercise, intellectual pursuits, and attitudes. One's life style has a lot to do with longevity and with individual health in old age. The idea, then, is to "die young" at an old age.

Exposure to pollution, exercise patterns, smoking behavior, alcohol consumption, and other aspects of life style can affect health and longevity. Diseases that reduce death age are frequently related to conditions that people bring on themselves. High fat and carbohydrate diets, sedentary life style, cigarette smoking, high caloric intake, and air pollution are widely known to contribute to poor health. Improvements in such environmental conditions, largely inherent in one's life style, have the potential of increasing life expectancy and improving personal health in old age.

An active life, with regular exercise an integral part of

everyday living, prolongs many physical capacities. Even muscle tone and strength can be regained by exercise among older men and women. Certain aging processes (e.g., atheromatous plaque formation) and the risk of coronary artery disease are also reduced; pulmonary functioning and related stimulation of the brain by oxygen are improved by exercise.

Changes in diet and nutrition alone cannot extend the life span, but can improve health and resistance to diseases. Moderate caloric consumption and increases in minerals, proteins, and vitamins may have many benefits in avoiding age-related disorders. Low cholesterol and total fat intake reduce the risk of coronary disease; increased calcium and protein consumption abate bone tissue deterioration. Proteins and vitamins also head off confusion, fatigue, irritability, insomnia, and "senility." Diet can prevent loss of teeth and dental diseases common among old people.

The effects of cigarette smoking and air pollution are widely known. Quitting smoking can improve respiratory and cardiovascular conditions. It also prevents nicotine from damaging blood vessels. There is a twofold increase in the overall death rate of smokers over nonsmokers in the 45 to 55 age bracket. The differences diminish somewhat thereafter because of other health and aging factors.

FUNCTIONAL AGE

Because life style and environmental conditions, heredity, and disease affect individuals in different ways, generalizations about aging and performance capacities cannot be applied fairly to specific individuals. Certainly chronological age is a poor indicator of aging. Generalities about the capabilities of specific age groups may represent "averages" and may be characteristic of some group members, but they constitute invalid stereotypes when applied to all group members.

Also, in the complex process of aging, individuals may have certain outstanding strengths and qualities that continue to improve with age (e.g., intelligence). Capacities relate to individual conditions and diseases, which form a configuration unique to each individual. Further, as some capacities diminish, others may be enhanced. For example, improved skill, judgment, and endurance may compensate for reduced speed of reaction or dexterity.

Hence, evaluation of the physical capacities of an individual must be conducted without relying on the person's chronological age. Rather, it should be conducted with reference to specified requirements of tasks to be performed, as discussed in Chapter 12. *Functional age* is determined by the individual's ability to perform required duties efficiently and safely (McFarland, 1976).

Measurement of functional age has not been explored as fully as one might think. The major progress has been in the area of evaluating physical fitness. Many studies conducted at The Fatigue Laboratory at Harvard University revealed changes in functional age resulting from different types of work in industry and the methods of maintaining functional fitness (Horvath and Horvath, 1973). Similarly, the Royal Canadian Air Force Tests and further development of these tests (Cooper, 1970) indicate how certain diseases can be prevented or controlled through stress tests. The work of Dr. Leon Koyl in measuring functional criteria for job placement (GULHEMP, as discussed in Chapter 12), is also noteworthy as pioneering research in functional age measurement (Koyl, 1970; Skinner and Quirk, 1973).

Various studies and experiments have been conducted to apply the concept of functional age assessment. These include warehouse workers in Aer Lingus (Irish Air Lines), clerical workers in the U.S. Civil Service, air transport pilots in the United States, automobile drivers, naval aviators, and industrial workers. These studies are reviewed by McFarland (McFarland, 1976).

With the new federal requirements that employment decisions be based on abilities to perform, and not on chronological age, interest is likely to increase in the subject of functional age assessment. We all know of individuals who are more capable than their age might suggest and of others who are "prematurely senile." Although we may give lip service to recognition of individual abilities without regard to age, we still tend to rely on stereotypes of aging, to generalize. We also recognize individuals who have some strengths but suffer from other infirmities that are used to exclude them from normal employment.

The increased application of the functional age concept will lead us to consider the specific abilities of older employees. We should not exaggerate the limiting effects of disease and chronic conditions, nor of the effects of aging itself. We should consider physical aspects of aging as a complex of variables that need to be analyzed for a fair evaluation of individual capabilities.

Successful adaptation in aging requires reconstruction by a person of essential psychological assets. The process requires reduced dependence and increased self-reliance, which leads to a stronger self-concept as an able person, which then leads to building and maintenance of further capacity to cope with the stresses of aging. This leads to further reduced susceptibility to negative external forces and thus further reduced dependence and increased self-reliance (Kuypers and Bengston, 1973; Bengston, 1973).

There is no reason why old age needs to be the "scrap heap" of life. More flexible retirement timing, supportive counseling by managers and specialists, and a more constructive attitude toward the transition to retirement or work in old age would aid individual adaptation. Old age may never be the "golden years," because of health and other problems, but psychological adaptation may certainly be made more effective.

CHAPTER TWELVE

PSYCHOLOGICAL ADAPTATION TO AGING

People who no longer have a necessary role to play in the social and economic life of their society generally deteriorate rapidly. The pattern of increasingly early retirement in our own society takes a heavy toll on our older citizens—Alexander Leaf, "Getting Old," *Scientific American.*

Just as disease has a significant effect on individual capacities in old age, so it has a significant effect on personality, emotions, and social relationships. Old people are often described as irritable, mean-tempered, rigid, forgetful, and slow. They may suffer from anxiety, depression, grief, and frequent paranoia. But many of these qualities, where they do exist, are related to physical conditions. They also frequently relate to personality patterns displayed earlier in life and to stresses brought on by changes in relationships with other people.

Aging, then, is not so much a condition to be "cured" as a process of life that requires adaptation by individuals. Just as the transition from adolescence to adulthood is a difficult transition for many people, so is the transition from middle age to old age. Clearly, most individuals have the intellectual capacity to deal with the stresses of growing old. Learning, memory, perception, judgment, and interactive capacities do not diminish significantly, and they may even strengthen as older persons draw on them to compensate for other losses. The key, then, is individual understanding of the psychological changes affecting their lives. Successful adaptation can then follow, allowing a person to live a satisfying "last third of life."

This chapter describes the principal social and emotional changes that affect individual adaptation to old age. From a management point of view, the psychological factors in work or retirement after the age of 65 can be as important as the physical competencies to perform. To feel old, useless, and unwanted is to be old, useless, and unwanted. The end of mandatory retirement impels management to be more understanding and supportive of older employees who are trying to adapt to changes occurring in their lives.

SOCIAL AGE FACTORS

Age is a social phenomenon. The notion of counting birthdays was invented as a simple and convenient way to classify people into groups. Banning mandatory retirement among employers is hardly likely to eliminate the view our society takes of people who are 65 and older. Far from it; in fact, getting employees of different generations (often three, not just two) to work together effectively is felt to be a challenge for management.

Ours is a youth-oriented society. But the ADEA is a reflection of gradual change. It is not likely that older persons will soon be revered and granted authority and power as may have once been the case in American history, but at least there is a greater recognition of the rights of older people. Birthdays are still counted, and stereotypes of older people persist. As a person grows older, he or she must cope with the social indignities that continue to be common in our society.

But what is old? Functional age is difficult to measure and is not a socially useful tool (although it offers considerable promise for specific employer applications). Simply, old is in the eye of the beholder. A person who is 58 and retired is viewed as "older" than a person 68 and still working actively. Bald heads, wrinkled skin, dress habits, job titles, and rank may all serve as indicators of social age.

Social perceptions of age suggest guidelines to people regarding how they should behave. Just as parents quit the PTA when their kids leave school, people are "supposed" to change their ways as they grow old. Social norms suggest that older people should be more interested in their family, church, hobbies, community activities, and personal financial independence than other age groups (Rosow, 1973).

"It's heck to get old" because of the ways others in society regard older people. For many, old age itself is a stigma, with more negative than positive characteristics. "On the basis of their age, older people are usually relegated to a position in society in which they are no longer judged to be of any use or importance" (Atchley, 1972). Negative attitudes toward aging may be wrong, but they persist, and social stereotypes can make life miserable for people who do not adapt effectively and maintain personal integrity in the process.

LIFE STAGES

Behavioral scientists have a term called "age grading." This means that our society has identified and perpetuated arbitrary divisions of the life cycle. Gail Sheehy's *Passages*, based in part on the theories of psychologist Daniel Levinson, appealed to a large popular market by characterizing stages of life that are commonly experienced. Sheehy talks of an "age thirty transition," "rooting," a "mid-life transition," and after the age of 45, a "restabilization and flowering." Her writing focused more on the mid-life "crisis" than on the adaptation to old age.

Actually, considerable research has been conducted on life cycles or life stages. But because of the variation of aging patterns and life styles, it is difficult to "prove" any particular theory of the life cycle. Life stages are models based on social perceptions and are useful to the extent that they further research and aid individuals in the orderly transition and adaptation through life.

When life expectancy was short and people worked their whole lives, the notion of life stages was without meaning. The concept of adolescence, for example, did not take on meaning until the late 1800s, and did not become widespread in social parlance until the 1900s (it has been traced to Rousseau's *Emile*, first published in 1762). Within the past few decades middle age has become clearly delineated (and people now know they have both a life stage here and a reason for socially acceptable crises). Middle age and old age are due to increasing longevity and improved health, but also due to earlier family rearing and earlier retirement.

The division of the "old" phase of life is the latest phenomenon. The young-old have emerged to differentiate from the old-old. Again, this is due to both longevity and earlier retirement ages. The young-old are relatively vigorous and healthy, relatively comfortable in economic terms, and relatively free from work and parental responsibilities (Neugarten, 1974). These categorizations are rooted in perceptions that have evolved in our contemporary society, not in fixed biological or psychological patterns of aging.

Of various life-stage theories proposed, old age is typically neglected. Eric Erikson (1968) refers to it as a period of maturity, or "ego integrity." Super (1957) and Hall and Nougaim (1968) refer to the stage as maintenance (and retirement). Miller and Form (1951) refer to the 45–64 stage as maintenance, followed by decline (deceleration and retirement). Campbell (1974) identifies a period of "regained serenity" after the age of 50, followed by "tidying up" after the age of 60. Sheehy (1976) suggests that after resolving the mid-life crisis, old age looks good—a stage of "restabilization and flowering." None gives specific, in-depth consideration of the complexities of adaptation to aging, but in probably a very real sense, each reflects a social perception of the life cycle and the relative role of old age.

THE RETIREMENT TRANSITION

Although life stage models usually indicate time frames bounded by years of age, the proponents usually acknowledge that individual differences are great. A major stress occurs when social forces push a person into a life stage transition when the person is not ready.

Retirement is a difficult transition, compounded when it is perceived to be forced. The Committee on Aging of the American Medical Association observed:

> At a certain chronological age—most often 65—forces outside of medicine inflict a disease or disability-producing condition upon working men and women that is no less devastating than cancer, tuberculosis, or heart disease. Compulsory retirement robs those affected of the will to live full, well-rounded lives, encourages atrophy and decay.

> Compulsory retirement on the basis of age will impair the health of many individuals whose job represents a major source of status, creative satisfaction, social relationships, or self-respect. It will be equally disastrous for the individual who works only because he has to, and who has a minimum of meaningful goals or interests in life, job-related or otherwise. Job separation may well deprive such a person of his

only source of identification and leave him floundering in a motivational vacuum with no frame of reference whatsoever.

There is ample clinical evidence that physical and emotional problems can be precipitated or exacerbated by denial of employment opportunities. Few physicians deny that a direct relationship exists between enforced idleness and poor health (Select Committee on the Aging, 1977).

In his Pulitzer Prize–winning book, *Why Survive? Being Old in America*, Butler (1975) characterized these effects as the "retirement syndrome." Although all retirees do not automatically suffer from anxiety and depression, many men and women who are otherwise healthy develop headaches, gastrointestinal symptoms, oversleeping, nervousness, irritability, nervousness, and lethargy in connection with retirement (Butler, 1975).

The depressions and anxieties of older people are due also to the loss or absence of close friends and to physical maladies experienced. Psychological testing of older persons indicates they tend to be more passive, defensive, depressed, and seclusive (Savage, 1972; Britton and Savage, 1965). One researcher reported that increased depression is common but expected in old age, given the withdrawal of the older person from society (Johnson, 1976).

After the age of 65 there is a sharp increase in alcohol and drug abuse. Many older people apparently try to medicate themselves for increased depression. Medically, drugs and alcohol have greater effect on older persons, and normally smaller dosages are required. Hence alcohol consumption and drug abuse are compounded problems (Baugher, 1977). It has also been observed that a moderate drinker will become, after retirement, a chronic drinker when cocktail parties replace employment-related activities (O'Meara, 1977).

Suicides also increase with age. One of four suicides in the United States is committed by a person 65 or over, even though the group represents only one in ten persons. And this is probably a low estimate, as families are reluctant to report deaths as such. The rates are highest for white males in this group (Harris, 1978).

OTHER STRESSES

Of course, loss of employment is not the only stress giving rise to these behaviors. Loss of family and friends, declining health, loss of social status, loss of self-esteem, marital difficulties or loss of spouse, and financial, housing, and legal problems contribute to psychological states that come up to be less than enthusiastic.

The death of a spouse is the most stressful event that can happen to a person. About half of all women over the age of 65 are widowed; one-fifth of men over 65 have lost their wives through death. In addition, many others have suffered bereavement from death of other relatives, close friends, colleagues, and children. The emotional and mental strains are typically severe and often difficult for older persons to bear. In addition to the inability to replace the spouse and the ending of a long relationship, the weakened physical condition of older persons makes adaptation difficult (Kimmel, 1974; Harris, 1978).

Marital difficulties are also often severe in old age, especially as compounding factors with the loss of employment and friends at work. Long-standing marital conflicts persist and may become more open when exacerbated by income loss, changes in living arrangements, etc. Strains of illness of one or both partners place demands not easily satisfied. Feelings of frustration, bitterness, "being wasted," and outright hostility (taken out on the spouse) may be vented (Harris 1978).

But stresses are not unique to older people. Sheehy's writings are full of anecdotes about stresses experienced by people as they grow older. Social scientists have long observed the effects of stresses such as rapid cultural change, failure, frustration, interpersonal competition, learning tasks, battle conditions, concentration camp confinement, impending surgery, acute and chronic illnesses, isolation, and job demotion (Mechanic, 1968).

In our society the age of 65 has become something of a watershed. From there life is reputed to be downhill. When a major personal stress occurs, such as the death of one's spouse, losing status in one's career, relocating to a new community, or losing contact with one's close friends, the shock effects are great. Because of the arbitrary age that has long been applied, many individuals have brought on the stresses voluntarily, albeit naively. To retire and move to Leisure World is following a norm, but can result in serious stress.

More flexible retirement policies, with earlier or deferred retirement, eases the strain on older employees. Stresses may be minimized in force and controlled in impact and timing. Some are unpredictable and uncontrollable; but research indicates that orderly, planned retirement minimizes this risk as well. Individuals who anticipate and plan for retirement tend to adapt more readily and find retirement far more satisfying.

SELF-CONCEPT

The attitude a person has concerning himself (herself) seems to have a lot to do with the degree of stress experienced as a person grows older. Persons who are able to accept the facts of physical aging are less likely to suffer mental and emotional illnesses relating to declining capacities. Persons who understand the roles played in their lives and are able to accept the need for role changes and successfully implement these role changes are more likely to have a positive outlook.

Self-concept involves a person's identity (Erikson, 1968) and this is something which is never complete or maintained once and for all. Identity in a social context is always open to change and development over time. Persons who are sensitive to personal life stages and the changing views that others have of them are able to adapt more effectively than persons who rigidly hold to identities they hold dear but which are obsolete. It is tough, for example, for a mother to stop mothering and a manager to stop managing. But healthy aging requires dropping of some roles in behavior in favor of others and the continuing development of one's identity.

In a study of self-concept and roles during old age, Cavan (1962) reports:

> At the point of compulsory retirement . . . the means of carrying out the social role disappears: the man is a lawyer without a case, a bookkeeper without books, a machinist without tools. Second, he is excluded from his group of former co-workers: as an isolated person he may be completely unable to function in his former role. Third, as a retired person, he begins to find a different evaluation of himself in the minds of others from the evaluation he had as an employed person. He no longer sees respect in the eyes of former subordinates, praise in the faces of former superiors, and approval in the manner of former co-workers. The looking glass composed of his former important groups throws back a changed image: he is done for, an old-timer, old-fashioned, on the shelf (pp. 527–528).

Flexible retirement may reduce the stresses associated with major role changes and subsequent changes in self-concept. On the other hand, it may allow individuals to avoid facing up to such necessary changes. Open communications (frankness included) are helpful in making older persons sensitive to changing role demands and perceptions of others. Passivity toward older workers is not helpful and does a disservice to individuals who assume life will continue on as in the past. Informal counseling by managers, peers, and other staff members can provide cues to individuals. Formal counseling and group discussions can help individuals realize the needs for change and guide them in developing changing role behaviors and self-concepts.

PATTERNS OF AGING: A SUMMARY

Too often, age is thought of as something unfortunate that befalls people. Either you're old or you're not. If you're not, you're young and athletic and adaptable; if you're old, you're part of the "Geritol set" and have one foot in the grave. Such black-and-white stereotypes are exaggerated, but they are, in fact, exaggerated in life. The end of mandatory retirement calls for a more enlightened view of aging and for management practices that are considerate and helpful to employees as they age.

"Age is best seen as the cumulation of developmental events at a particular point of time in the life of an individual," reports a gerontologist (Bengston, 1973). Chronological age is an arbitrary yardstick that is often meaningless in characterizing what a person can and cannot do and what a person feels and wants. Each individual has a unique time clock governing physical aging, psychological adjustment to aging, and emotions. Views of "age" are as much a result of social perceptions as they are on determinate biological conditions of an individual. Thus we need to be very attentive to individual differences as we judge abilities to perform, as we advise regarding career steps and retirement, and as we influence the circumstances in which we interact with persons of different ages.

A common-sense theory of aging holds that old age is not all that much different from middle age, with the exception of biological and health changes. The "activity theory" of aging assumes that older people are expected to continue to be active and to compensate for loss of work or friends or spouse by increasing activities with other people. The self-concept, sources of satisfaction, and life style are not expected to change much. The rugged American individualist can survive aging by striving to "wear out," not "rust out."

A very different view of aging is presented by a "disengagement theory." Older people are seen as inevitably letting go of middle-age attitudes, values, and activities—withdrawing psychologically and socially from the environment. And the process of disengagement is viewed as satisfying because it releases older persons from societal pressures and stressful activities. This theory emphasizes the importance of change —of individual development—with increasing age. Successful adaptation to aging requires psychological, physiological, and social changes. Withdrawal is natural, inevitable, and functional for society—it allows younger people to assume social roles and responsibilities (Cumming and Henry, 1961).

In reality, some people wear out, some rust out, and some burn out. There is truth in each view of aging and psychological adaptation to aging. Many people may tend to disengage in response to stressful events and to physical aging. But for many, keeping involved and active is highly important for maintenance of self-concept and for continued life satisfaction. Indeed, continued activity helps sustain good health as well as positive psychological adaptation in aging. As one researcher noted:

> People, as they grow old, seem to be neither at the mercy of the social environment nor at the mercy of some set of intrinsic processes—in either instance, inexorable changes that they cannot influence. On the contrary, the individual seems

to continue to make his own "impress" upon the wide range of social and biological changes. He continues to exercise choice and to select from the environment in accordance with his own long-established needs. He ages according to a pattern that has a long history, and that maintains itself, with adaptation, to the end of life (Neugarten, 1968).

PART FIVE

HELPING EMPLOYEES
PLAN FOR RETIREMENT

CHAPTER THIRTEEN

THE RETIREMENT EXPERIENCE: ATTITUDES AND LIFE STYLES

I had no objections to relinquishing my duties to younger men, as their youth and enthusiasm were needed. At 65, I felt the need for a complete change in pace, occupation, interests, and to a place of cleaner air and better climate. I am enjoying a full life in southern Florida—Retired technical sales representative, Eastman Kodak Company.

Not everyone moves to Florida when they retire. Many of Kodak's retirees live around Rochester, New York, the company's home base. Neither are all retirees happy in retirement, but 95% of 1500 retirees surveyed by Kodak said they were. Most often, they cited good health and adequate income as the reasons for their contentment. Only 12% of the respondents said that they or their spouses had serious health problems. Nearly 70% said their retirement income is enough or more than enough, although inflation was a major concern.

Knowing how retirees feel about their retirement and their retirement conditions can be helpful to an employer. Understanding why employees retire when they do, whether they are satisfied in retirement and why, whether they seek work after retirement, and other factors in retirement attitudes and style are important determinants of company retirement policies and programs. Too often, companies

second-guess employees, assuming that if the pension benefits were liberalized, more employees would retire earlier.
Maybe so, but that is a simplistic way to manage such an
important personnel process.

This chapter examines employee attitudes and experiences in retirement and suggests ways surveys of retirees
may be conducted to guide management actions. Results
from a survey of 1585 retirees from seven major corporations
are briefly discussed as a suggested starting point for conducting a company survey.

WHAT IS SUCCESSFUL RETIREMENT?

Issues of *Harvest Years* and *Retirement Living* regularly
offer features on how to retire "successfully." Such magazine
articles are aimed at the prospective retiree and the recent
retiree and are often made available to individuals by employers. The focus of attention is on such questions as: In
retirement, will you have enough money for your needs?
How will you readjust your budget? Do you plan to work?
Should you move to another climate or to a smaller home?

One such article offers "ten secrets for successful retirement" for the prospective retiree (Alpert, 1973). The points
discussed include:

- Know exactly what your finances are.
- Get a complete health checkup.
- Consider whether you really need a car.
- Replace outmoded or defective major appliances (particu-
larly if you plan to relocate).
- Consider your housing and leisure plans: should you move?
- Don't move because it's where the children are.
- Pick a trusted attorney.
- "Test-run" your retirement on weekends.

Other articles suggest abrupt replacement of one's doctor and lawyer with younger persons—who can "take care of you when you are old." Some advocate a change of location to help get a new retirement life started; others advocate staying close to friends and familiar places. Some dwell on the importance of saving money and wisely investing one's nest egg for income and preservation of assets. Others downplay the financial importance of retirement, as it is only one factor influencing feelings in retirement.

Financial worries may be very realistic and very important for employees (such as industrial workers). One researcher bluntly observed, "a favorable preretirement attitude toward retirement is in large measure dependent upon the expected retirement income" (Thompson, 1958). But executives and employees covered by adequate retirement benefit programs may not be so concerned with retirement income as with postretirement activities and the loss of work. Conversely, an assumed importance of work as a primary source of meaning and satisfaction in life may be partially a result of upper-middle-class orientations.

It is difficult to generalize about what constitutes successful or satisfying retirement. Research suggests, however, that employees who expect a positive retirement experience are likely to have a positive attitude toward retirement; if their expectations are realistic, that is the way their retirement is likely to be. With that profound observation, it is then necessary to consider how individual differences shape up. The retirement experience depends on an individual's circumstances and individual expectations and desires relating to retirement (Glamser, 1976).

PURPOSES OF RETIREE SURVEYS

Eastman Kodak surveyed 2500 retirees (1500 responded) to help the company "more clearly understand the needs and life styles of retirees as Kodak continues to review its plans and benefits." At the time of the survey, however, no changes in the retirement plan were contemplated, although an increase had recently been granted to all of Kodak's retired employees. Other companies have conducted similar surveys, primarily to test the perceived adequacy of retirement benefits provided but also to keep in communication with retirees.

In other organizations surveys are conducted to broaden the base of information available on pensioners and annuitants. The Civil Service Commission has conducted periodic surveys of retirees. Also, TIAA-CREF, the retirement income agency serving educational institutions, conducted a survey of 2269 annuitants aged 60 and over. An earlier survey had been conducted in 1948. The TIAA survey gathered objective data on finances, housing, health, employment, mobility, and other aspects of retirement living and also narrative data. The open-ended questions asked respondents for comments on problems they had faced in retirement and an evaluation of their retirement experience. In this study, as in most others, responses were kept anonymous (Mulanaphy, 1974; Ingraham, 1974). The results of the two aspects of the TIAA-CREF survey were published in separate volumes.

As a rule, retirees provide a high rate of response. The response to the TIAA survey was 70%. Kodak obtained a 60% response rate. In other studies response rates have typically been above 50%. There may be truth in the common observation that retirees have plenty of time to fill out questionnaires. But it is apparent also that respondents are eager to "tell it like it is," and surveys are a direct media for communicating with the world.

Other surveys have been conducted for the purpose of studying retirement patterns, particularly early retirement patterns (Greene, 1969; Barfield and Morgan, 1969).

A number of sample questionnaires for surveying retiree

attitudes and experiences are provided in *Retirement in American Society* (Streib and Schneider, 1971). The book also presents the results of a study conducted by researchers at Cornell University over a period of years. The longitudinal nature of the study permitted analysis of the changes occurring in attitudes, thus revealing the dynamics of retirement experiences over time. The items in the questionnaires, however, may be used by an employer in surveying retiree attitudes.

THE TPF&C SURVEY

A survey was conducted in 1974 by TPF&C, a management consulting firm, to explore reactions to early retirement practices. The study began with interviews with executives in 28 large corporations in the United States and Canada. These interviews provided information on company policies and practices, with particular attention given early retirement programs for executives (TPF&C, 1974; Walker, 1975). Seven of these companies also participated in a questionnaire survey of retirees.

The corporations provided mailing lists of retirees and a questionnaire was sent to all of the retirees, a total of 2563 persons. The responses were sent directly to TPF&C and numbered 1585, with 1486 usable responses (a response rate of 58%). It included questions concerning demographic factors, the decision to retire, the extent of preparation for retirement, income, health, activities, attitudes about retired life, and the Retirement Description Index (RDI) developed by Smith, Kendall, and Hulin (1969). Many of the questions were adapted from items previously used by Hunter, Manion, and others.

Analysis of the results suggests that retiring voluntarily is a more important determinant of retirement satisfaction than is timing. Many retirees who reported they were forced to retire had less positive attitudes than those who retired voluntarily, and they were distinctly less satisfied on the four key dimensions: health, finances, activities and work, and associations with people. Multivariate analysis indicated that health and preretirement feelings about retiring were more important than timing of retirement when it comes to assessing retirement satisfaction. Similarly, health, preretirement feelings, and financial status all were more important determinants of satisfaction than the voluntary or nonvoluntary nature of the retirement decision. However, when these factor are held constant, nonvoluntary retirement decisions were clearly associated with lower retirement satisfaction. Also, for those who felt forced to retire (nonvoluntary retirees), timing remained a significant predictor of satisfaction (Kimmel, Price, and Walker, 1977; Walker, Price, and Kimmel, 1978).

As indicated in Table 1, presenting responses to certain questions regarding reactions to retirement, a diversity of attitudes were displayed in the study sample. The analyses sorted the group by demographic factors, company level (title), retirement timing, retirement choice, and other variables. Multiple regression allowed further examination of the diverse responses in relation to the attitudinal responses and the specific RDI scores. The executives in the sample (140 individuals who held an officer title and had a salary in excess of $50,000 at the time of retirement) displayed more positive attitudes than the total sample in virtually all aspects of retirement satisfaction. But this group also reported a higher percentage of voluntary retirement decisions (70% for executive group, 51% for the total sample).

Accordingly, the analyses of these survey data pointed up the fact of individual differences. To understand the retirement experience, including attitudes, activities, and satisfaction, we must break down our generalized characterizations

Table 1. Reactions to Retirement (%)

Description of Retirement	Strongly Agree	Agree	Disagree	Strongly Disagree
I have made many plans for things I'll be doing a month or years from now	18	45	33	4
The things I do are as interesting to me as they ever were	34	56	9	1
This is just about the dreariest time of my life	4	8	28	60
I expect some interesting and pleasant things to happen to me in the future	21	62	14	3
I often find a hard time keeping busy	4	13	38	45
As I grow older, things really seem better than I thought they would be	14	59	25	3
I am old and somewhat tired	2	14	45	39
My life is full of worry	2	7	45	45
People should retire only when they are no longer able to work	13	20	42	25
Retirement is generally good for a person	14	63	18	4

N = approximately 1500, varies with item responses.

of retirees. Detailed surveys by employers enable a more refined and more accurate picture of the feelings and needs of retirees. By gaining this knowledge, an employer may modify retirement inducements and practices so as to make retirement more satisfying in ways tailored to the actual situation.

RETIREMENT STYLES

Life style has a lot to do with the decision to retire and subsequent retirement satisfaction. With more flexible retirement timing, more employees will choose their timing and life style from a wider range of options. Many employees today look forward to retirement as an opportunity to move away from a working career and turn to other pursuits, whether leisure, postretirement work activities, or rest. To provide a more meaningful focus in discussions of retirement decision and adaptation patterns and their implications for employer policies and practices, it is helpful to consider different types of retirement styles.

Four retirement styles were examined through the TPF&C survey data (Walker, Price, and Kimmel, 1978). These styles reflect previous research on retirement which considered retirement styles (Neugarten, Havighurst and Tobin, 1968; Reichard, Livson and Peterson, 1962). The focus in the types of styles considered is on work-related retirement activities and not on personality traits:

Reorganizer: These are the people who engage in many types of pursuits. They tend to substitute new activities for the work they left behind, often becoming quite active in voluntary activities. They continue to be active in life, but in a newly reorganized life pattern. These "young at heart" retirees tend to plan ahead, be in better health, and have better financial condition than others. They are often found living in Leisure

World, actively engaged in shuffleboard tourneys and involved in other satisfying activities.

Holding On: These persons do not accept aging or the need for retirement. They are highly active and want to continue working indefinitely. They tend to be in good health and feel they need to continue earning money. These persons are largely responsible for the pressures resulting in state and federal legislation banning mandatory retirement. There may be many Grey Panthers among them.

Rocking Chair: These persons prefer a reduced level of life activity. They pose the classic image of the graceful, tired, disengaged folks. They are generally satisfied with their decline in activity and have made the intentional decision to disengage from the pace of life without giving up. They typically retire "on time," go to retirement preparation programs, and may be the people who most enjoy Lawrence Welk reruns.

Dissatisfied: These persons are usually in poor health, have low retirement income, are inactive, apathetic, and quiet. They have a difficult time adjusting to retirement, but in many instances they had a hard time adjusting to their work, too. They are the employees whom you never noticed when they were working, and did not notice when they retired. They tend to be unhappy in retirement, having left work when forced out.

Granted, these four generalizations merely replace one generalization. But the point is that individual differences in circumstances and attitudes toward retirement need to be taken into account. Not all employees are "grey panthers," eager to stay on until they drop on their jobs. Neither are all retirees eager to start a life anew.

Table 2 presents a summary of the principal characteristics of these four retirement styles, as revealed through the survey data analysis.

Table 2. Four Retirement Styles

	"Reorganizer"	"Holding On"	"Rocking Chair"	"Dissatisfied"
Sample of 1341 Retirees	24%	19%	44%	13%
Retirement style	Highly active, but in a newly *reorganized* lifestyle (voluntary activities, perhaps also working for pay)	Highly active, want to continue *working* indefinitely	Reduced life activity but satisfied with present level of activity	Not working and feel it's difficult to keep busy
Preretirement attitude	Just waiting to retire to start a new pattern of activities	Most had not thought of retiring; were asked to retire	Looked forward to it (relief from work)	Many had no thoughts of it and were forced to retire; would like to work but can't
Overall satisfaction with retirement	Highest satisfaction; view retirement as positive life stage	Negative view of retirement; satisfaction is high since they are working *after* retirement	Moderately high overall; but satisfaction reduced by health problems	Least positive attitude toward retired life; lowest on all scales of satisfaction
Health	Better health	Better health	Poorer health	Poorest health

Retirement timing and choice	Tend to be on-time (62–65); choice usually voluntary, well planned, and for positive reasons	Tend to be early, perceived as involuntary or for negative reasons; more likely to have been unexpected	Tend to be on-time (62–65); voluntary	Tend to be on-time (62–65)
Education and financial status	Usually more educated; higher occupational status and income before retirement	Often technical and professional people; low preretirement income	Satisfied with present financial situation; average on other characteristics	Lowest education, poorest income and financial situation; many in sales or production jobs before retirement
Other	Would probably do retirement planning on their own	Youngest group; more dependents; one-third need income; most like working	Would probably attend retirement preparation counseling	Oldest group; highly dissatisfied; had been retired longest; depressed and frustrated

CHAPTER FOURTEEN

RETIREMENT PREPARATION

Preparation for retirement, in terms of developing options, really ought to begin very early, certainly if we are talking about transitions. Retirement is more than simply economics, it has to do with a whole way of life, with wanting to get up in the morning—Arthur N. Schwartz, Psychologist, University of Southern California Ethel Percy Andrus Gerontology Center.

With all of the discussion of the federal age amendments and the pros and cons of raising mandatory retirement age, many employees may be confused about their own retirement plans. Some will surely misapprehend the facts and be anxious about retirement:

- "Will I have to work until 70 even if I don't want to?"

- "Will I be better off financially if I stay around as long as I can?"

- "Can I start collecting Social Security while I'm still working?"

- "If I retire and then work for someone else, will I lose my pension benefits?"

These are the kinds of questions that the recent legislation might raise in employees' minds. In California and Florida, where legislation prohibiting mandatory retirement for all employees at any age has been enacted, these questions are particularly important to employees.

Communications and other assistance to employees in preparing for retirement can help answer these and other questions. At a very minimum, a company should explain to employees what the new retirement-age laws mean to them and how company policies and practices are likely to be affected. A positive, constructive, and enlightened viewpoint from the company can go a long way toward reassuring employees who are facing the retirement decision. Also, a company should be sure that employees are fully aware of their benefits, both pension and insurance, at normal and early retirement. ERISA summary plan descriptions are probably not adequate to do all of this. Special publications, letters, articles in house organs, speeches, and group meetings are all possible ways to keep in touch with employees as the implications of a changing retirement age ceiling takes effect.

But management assistance needs to go beyond one-way communications regarding benefits and the effects of legislative and policy changes. Delegates at a recent White House Conference on Aging asserted that, "Every employer has a major responsibility for providing preparation for retirement programs. Management has a vested interest in such programs." If funds invested in pension and profit sharing plans are to be utilized as intended, a companion program of retirement preparation should be provided.

This chapter discusses typical retirement preparation programs offered by companies and evaluates their effectiveness. Suggestions are provided for designing and conducting retirement preparation programs. Further, possible new approaches are discussed, integrating retirement preparation into longer-range career development planning beginning at mid-career for employees.

ORIGINS OF PROGRAMS

Retirement preparation has its origins in the function of explaining to employees upon retirement of their pension benefits and insurance coverages. A 1950 survey by The Equitable Life Assurance Society showed that only 13% of 355 companies had preretirement programs of one kind or another. A 1952 survey by Hewitt and Associates covered 657 companies with a work force of 2.5 million. All size and industrial classifications were represented, but with a bias toward large manufacturers. The study found that interviews were the common method used and that most interviews emphasized the probable amount of pension benefit and optional settlement, if any. Only 2.7% of the companies offered educational or lecture programs regarding retirement (Hunter, 1962).

Pioneering work in developing broader, more formal retirement preparation programs was performed by the University of Michigan, the University of Chicago, and several large private employers. The works of Professor Woodrow Hunter at Michigan, Donald Bowman at Drake University, Vincent Manion and others at the University of Oregon, and Richard Barfield and James Morgan at the University of Michigan (working with the auto workers) have all contributed to increased prevalance of programs and improved program design and content over the years.

By the early 1970s various sources had developed materials useful to companies in assisting employees in retirement preparation. The Action for Independent Maturity (AIM), a division of the American Association of Retired Persons (AARP), published a series of booklets on such subjects as health, income, financial planning, use of time, housing and location, legal affairs, and attitude and role adjustment. AARP is mainly concerned with retirees; AIM with employees approaching retirement. Both also publish bimonthly magazines (*Dynamic Maturity* and *Modern Maturity*) and provide other services furthering retirement preparation.

The Manpower Education Institute publishes a manual to be used with a television program which it produces called "Ready or Not." Retirement Advisors, Inc. (RAI) is a private firm that provides written materials for house organs, a monthly newsletter to be sent to retirees, and a series of guidebooks for prospective retirees. *Retirement Living* is a monthly magazine published by a firm of the same name. An Oregon firm, Retirement Services, Inc. (RSI) has published a series of retirement preparation guides to be used in group employee discussions in preparation for retirement. Audiovisual materials have also been published, including "One Third of Your Life," a program tested by Don Bowman and researchers at Drake University's Preretirement Planning Center (funded for a time by the Department of Labor). Other organizations such as B'nai B'rith, the National Council on the Aging, the U.S. Social Security Administration, and local governmental agencies also have developed preretirement program materials and guidelines for providing such assistance to employees.

Apparently, there has been no shortage of published materials and guidelines for retirement preparation.

CURRENT PRACTICES

How have these materials been used? Are companies providing assistance to employees in areas other than purely financial matters? Are only the large companies providing assistance?

According to a Conference Board survey in 1974, most large corporations offer some form of assistance to prospective retirees. Of 800 responding companies, 704 offered some type of program. Of these, 371 limit their assistance to provision of financial information; a further 170 provide basic information on supplemental benefits available under company health insurance plans. An additional 163 provide more general counseling, although 60 of these merely supply written materials such as external publications. The remaining 193 companies provide counseling on a personal basis, making opportunities available for employees to discuss retirement problems with "people qualified to help them work out solutions" (O'Meara, 1974, 1977).

A 1976 survey by Prentice-Hall and ASPA (American Society for Personnel Administration) found that 75% of the responding 269 companies (of 1500 contacted) have preretirement planning programs. More than half offer individualized counseling; about one-third conduct group counseling sessions; and the remainder have both types of sessions available. A third of the companies responding planned to initiate additional programs by 1980 (Prentice-Hall, 1976).

These studies indicate that retirement preparation assistance in most companies is limited to financial and basic health insurance information. Assistance in other areas tends to be offered through individualized counseling. The surveys do not indicate whether the larger companies are predominantly those with formal programs, but other data indicate this is often so. Smaller companies typically have so few employees retiring each year that formal programs are not felt to be needed.

EXAMPLES OF COMPANY PROGRAMS

The many companies that have introduced retirement preparation programs provide examples of different approaches that can be taken. The following are examples gleaned from published accounts of the forms of retirement assistance provided to employees. Accordingly, some of the practices described may have been subsequently superceded.

AT&T: Through a company-sponsored organization, called the Telephone Pioneers of America, the company offers preretirement and postretirement employees with films, speakers, literature, and counseling.

IBM: Employees approaching retirement (as early as age 52) can receive $500 a year toward the costs of courses taken from educational institutions. The reimbursement is available for 3 years before retirement and 2 years after. The program was introduced in November 1976.

Chrysler Corporation: Since 1965 auto workers at Chrysler have been offered a free 7-week course relating to retirement. The costs are borne by the company and the UAW. Reportedly, a small percentage of eligible retirees opt to take the course, however.

Citicorp: Seminars are held periodically at the headquarters, where employees nearing retirement can learn about benefits, financial planning, and health matters. Additionally, eight smaller workshops are conducted with AIM materials. Here doctors, lawyers, Social Security specialists, and others are brought in as guest speakers.

Sears, Roebuck: An ombudsman was appointed to work full time with retirees, drawing on experts within and outside the company to solve problems troubling retirees.

Ampex Corporation: Eight 2-hour sessions on retirement issues are conducted by topical specialists. Additionally, for employees aged 45 to 55, an abbreviated 6-hour program is offered, with emphasis on financial planning. The 8-week program is available to all employees 45 and older.

Chemical Bank: Seminars are conducted by external specialists in preretirement counseling. Each enrolee is entitled to private counseling as well as the seminar.

TRW: A 12-week course is offered to retirees and spouses that includes discussion of psychological and sexual adjustment.

Zenith Radio Corporation: Eight seminars of 2 hours each are conducted, followed by personal counseling sessions.

Connecticut General: An 8-week series of meetings is held on company time and company premises.

Dow Chemical, Texas Power & Light, Koppers, Polaroid, Lockheed, Exxon, United Air Lines, American Airlines, Eastman Kodak, Lever Brothers, and General Electric are all among the companies cited as having such programs.

PROGRAMS FOR EXECUTIVES

As a rule, executives do not participate to the degree that other employee groups do. This may be due to their improved personal planning, to their reluctance to participate in formal programs with other employees, and perhaps to a greater self-confidence, reflecting a somewhat different set of needs to be satisfied.

Special programs tailored to the executive group usually focus on two subjects: financial planning and planning for a substitute for work (whether it be a second career, another job, or personal pursuits). Typically, assistance to executives is strictly personal counseling by external specialists (Kinzel, 1974). Such assistance was provided by numerous companies during the 1974–1975 recession, when early retirements for executives were likely to catch some individuals unprepared for sudden retirement.

Other than possible outplacement assistance for executives who wish to be reemployed, financial counseling is the primary focus. Numerous companies have instituted financial counseling as a perquisite for key executives. The service is paid for by the employer and provided by independent financial counseling firms (Teague, 1973; Perham, 1973). Some of the attraction of financial counseling has faded as the IRS has considered the perquisite to be taxable personal income, but it is, nevertheless, an important form of assistance to the executive anticipating retirement.

TYPICAL PROGRAM DESIGN

Company-sponsored programs cover pretty much the same ground. Figure 1 outlines the topical areas covered by the AIM guidebooks, which are representative of the majority of programs.

The Challenge of Retirement

Changes you'll want to make. How challenges create opportunities. Adding years to your life. Adding life to your years.

Health and Safety

How retirement will affect your health. The value of checkups. Exercise. Preventing medical problems. Nutrition. Safety.

Housing and Location

Where do people retire? Climate considerations? Cost of living? The choice of moving or not moving. How to move. Housing.

Legal Affairs

Obligations in transactions. Special retirement situations. When you may need a lawyer and how to choose one. Contracts, buying, selling, renting. Ownership. Wills and estates.

Attitudes and Role Adjustments

Change as a way of life. Humor. Shifting roles. Marriage risks. How to grandparent. Friendships. Being single. Late marriages.

Meaningful Use of Time

Leisure. What we want from the time we spend. Activities.

Sources and Amounts of Income

Where the money will come from. Emergency money, investment money, guaranteed money, extra money. Adequacy.

Financial Planning

Financial needs. What to spend money on. How to budget. Practical tips on cutting expenses. Early retirement?

Figure 1.   Topics for Retirement Preparation.

Participation is almost always voluntary, and groups are usually formed to be homogeneous (e.g., salaried employees, hourly workers). Traditionally, employees participate within 1 year of their scheduled (mandatory) retirement. The trend is toward earlier participation in the programs, with the norm being from 2 to 3 years before retirement.

Nonroutine topics are typically handled on a case-by-case basis in personal counseling. Use of leisure time, second careers or postretirement employment, and life-style adjustments are widely considered to be personal affairs and not a subject for open discussion with the company involved. Yet counseling necessarily is provided when employees seek assistance in these areas.

Most companies conduct the programs and provide counseling with their own staffs. Some use both in-house capabilities and outside specialists. Responsibility for retirement preparation used to rest with the benefits administration function, but it has shifted in many companies to broader employee relations, training, or career development functions. Benefits staff continue to have a large role to play, but involvement of other personnel staff tends to aid the coverage of nonfinancial subjects.

The principal objectives of such programs are to provide employees with current factual information on retirement matters, to encourage positive thinking about retirement, and to urge action on planning for retirement, particularly on attitudes, income budgeting and finances, legal matters, and planning for relocations and leisure. Companies are often concerned with the impressions remaining employees will have of the way retirees are treated (and feel as they leave). Also, many companies feel that retirement preparation is a social responsibility and a necessary benefit for long-service employees. Of course, the fact that other companies provide such programs is often a stimulus.

Guidelines are readily available to assist a company in designing and introducing a conventional retirement preparation program (Holley and Feild, 1974; Bartlett, 1974; Otte, 1974, O'Meara, 1977).

ARE THESE PROGRAMS ADEQUATE?

There has not appeared to be a compelling force for companies to invest significant attention or resources in retirement preparation. By and large it has been a low-budget, low-keyed, simplistic offering for those employees who express interest in it. Often, those who attend are those who need the assistance the least.

Because retirement is a paradox, retirement preparation needs to meet high standards. On the one hand, retirement is a reward for a long career of service—the "golden years"; on the other hand, it is the "scrap heap" of life—total and complete rejection from meaningful participation in the mainstream of life. To induce employees to retire in an era with no mandatory retirement age, companies need to stress the positive, attractive qualities of retirement. Getting old is "bad enough" without telling employees, however subtly, that they are through.

Without criticizing the fine programs offered by major companies today, it may be fair to characterize such programs at their worst. Employees of a certain age are invited to meet in the cafeteria Wednesday nights for 8 weeks to get some rather dull booklets and hear some rather dull speakers come and tell them how to live on half their income, how to decide whether to relocate and live in a mobile home in Florida, and how to find hobbies and new acquaintances so they won't miss all their friends at work so much. Also covered is how to cope with declining health, chronic disabilities common with aging, and imminent death. For some reason, writing a will takes on greater importance when you retire than 10 years before. A positive view of retirement?

A review of such programs by a researcher at the U.S.C. Gerontology Center concluded:

> The current lack of enthusiasm for retirement preparation programs traces back to the empirical evidence suggesting such programs are ineffective; i.e., by failing to change employees' attitudes toward work and retirement, they fail to perform their counseling functions. Several reasons for the participants' lack of substantial attitude changes have been highlighted, including the fundamental fact that the programs themselves are neither intensive enough nor properly designed to focus on such attitude changes as the basic goal. Without well-designed programs, objective evaluations of effectiveness are impossible to obtain. Lacking outstanding results, employers are reluctant to implement new programs or to revamp the old (Kasschau, 1974).

As illustrated in Figure 2, changing of attitudes is not something that is common in most programs today. Attitude

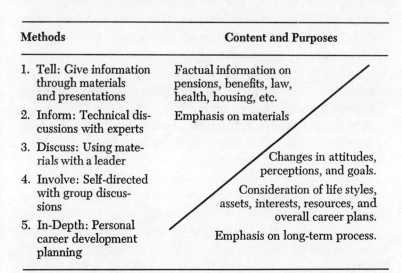

Methods	Content and Purposes
1. Tell: Give information through materials and presentations	Factual information on pensions, benefits, law, health, housing, etc.
2. Inform: Technical discussions with experts	Emphasis on materials
3. Discuss: Using materials with a leader	Changes in attitudes, perceptions, and goals.
4. Involve: Self-directed with group discussions	Consideration of life styles, assets, interests, resources, and overall career plans.
5. In-Depth: Personal career development planning	Emphasis on long-term process.

(Credit is due Donald G. Murray for concepts represented in this figure.)

Figure 2.   Aproaches for Retirement Preparation.

change and dealing with personal behavioral problems and plans requires a totally different approach than is applied in most retirement preparation programs today. Rather, today's programs concentrate on the disseminating of factual information considered by management to be pertinent to employees as they become retirees. The methods and the content are opposites.

Conventional retirement preparation programs seem to serve the limited purposes set forth, and they certainly are competitively adequate. From an employer's viewpoint they don't "rock the boat." Keeping programs simple and superficial minimizes risks of stirring up deeper employee problems which are their own responsibility to resolve. The Coca-Cola Company indicated to the *Wall Street Journal* that "We try to tread a cautious path of not interfering with an employee's life." The popularity of printed materials such as booklets and magazines (and now the more "advanced" casette and workbook programs) attests to the emphasis on information-giving and self-responsibility for planning.

The whole business of retirement preparation has taken too much of the "just a little and rather late" aura. The retirees who participate are told, by implication, that they need to get prepared, because they have a major shock coming. The tone of retirement preparation is anticipation of a sudden and major turning point in one's life.

The idea of flexible retirement, made reality with the passage of state and (to the age of 70) federal legislation, calls for a markedly different approach. There should be no retirement shock. There should be no need to get one's house in order. There certainly should be no marked transition. Companies stopped giving gold watches some time ago, but for reasons other than encouraging flexible retirement attitudes (would you believe inflation?). Many have also stopped featuring retirees in newsletters and in "last supper" banquets where they are bade farewell.

GUIDELINES FOR A CAREER DEVELOPMENT APPROACH

As discussed in previous chapters, aging is a gradual process, largely an emotional experience, health being a given. If individuals can be guided to adapt effectively to changing stresses as they grow older, the decision to retire may be made naturally and in a manner supportive of both employer and personal goals. Financial planning need not begin at 60, or even 50, or 40. It could be a way of life, as part of systematic overall career development planning. Similarly, the loss of work, declining abilities, and other stressful factors are not unique to the prospective retiree and may be incorporated in longer-range, broader career planning.

Granted, employees over the age of 55 and anticipating retirement may have certain information needs not considered pertinent earlier. These may be satisfied with materials and discussions, preferably within the context of self-initiated, realistic, in-depth career planning.

Career planning is a process of systematic self-analysis and action planning. If individuals are equipped to manage their own careers, the shocks of life transitions will be lessened. At the same time, human resource planning by an employer is eased through more thoughtful and rational personal career plans. Most people will retire at an appropriate time if they have the pertinent facts about their performance, their options, and the tools to consider personal interests and plans (Walker, 1973, 1976a, 1977b).

Career planning provides all employees with certain benefits:

■ Better direction and purpose. Screening of alternative career directions.

■ Better development action planning. Reasons for taking educational courses, doing reading, and undertaking other activities to build skills and knowledge.

- Better ability to initiate career changes. Better equipped to indicate desires to management and to make job changes and retirement with greater ease.

- Better preparedness to discuss career and performance matters with managers. Equipped to obtain counseling and feedback desired and to propose career actions based on in-depth planning.

A career planning approach to retirement preparation requires a total view of the individual (abilities and interests), the opportunities available (total retirement, gradual retirement, job changes, etc.), the demands of the present job (performance standards, changes, etc.), and the specific action plans to be implemented. The process is the same at any age, only the issues and facts vary. Young employees are more likely to be concerned with long-range career paths, compensation opportunities, and training and development programs. Older employees are more concerned with immediate job satisfaction, career redirections, "unfinished scripts" (as yet unfulfilled personal ambitions and desires), and understanding and adaptation regarding physical and emotional changes that are evolving.

The methods indicated in Figure 2 are applicable to career planning as an approach, but the emphasis would be on discussions and on self-directed learning with the use of materials and other career resources (references, workshops, counseling, etc.). The method of career planning calls for a comprehensive view of the older employee as an aspiring, talented, motivated, but often anxious person. Just as career planning helps younger employees access the company system and middle managers cope with the system, so career planning for older employees can help them survive in the system and to leave voluntarily at the time that is "right."

PART SIX

RESOURCES AND REFERENCES

CHAPTER FIFTEEN

WHERE TO GO FROM HERE

Congress should continue with the assistance of the Executive Branch to carefully study the issue of ending mandatory retirement in the non-Federal sector and to monitor the impact of the changes resulting from the enactment of H.R. 5383—*Mandatory Retirement: The Social and Human Cost of Enforced Idleness.*

This book has raised numerous points that should be considered by an employer in adopting and implementing new retirement-age policies. Yet the experience base on which advice is offered is quite limited. Few companies have managed without mandatory retirement ages. It is not yet known how many employees will want to stay on after age 65 or whether the employees that stay on are the better or the poorer performers. Broadly, it is not known what effects higher retirement ages will have on unemployment, Social Security, or productivity.

The sources cited throughout this book represent a valuable source of information and ideas potentially useful to the employer in dealing with these uncertain future conditions. Although no single reference provides ready answers to troubling questions, the research and observations of specialists in gerontology, human resource management, economics, sociology, and other fields may provide a rational foundation for management decision making. This chapter reviews, by way of a summary, the books considered by the authors to be most worthy of management attention.

RETIREMENT AGE

Anyone interested in pursuing the subject of retirement age further should obtain a copy of the report by the Select Committee on Aging (House of Representatives), entitled "Mandatory Retirement: The Social and Human Cost of Enforced Idleness." It may be obtained from the Superintendent of Documents, U.S. Government Printing Office, Washington, D.C. 20402 (Comm. Pub. No. 95–91, August 1977). It provides the primary facts and arguments that underly the 1978 legislation. It is an excellent synopsis of the pertinent issues relating to the law and the effects of mandatory retirement on people.

Also of related interest are the published proceedings of a hearing held December 10, 1976 before the Subcommittee on Retirement Income and Employment. Entitled "Age and Sex Discrimination in Employment and Review of Federal Response to Employment Needs of the Elderly," the publication includes statements by Dr. Arthur Flemming, Chairman of the Commission on Civil Rights, and Michael D. Batten, an industrial gerontologist. Mr. Batten is associated with the Manpower Institute in Washington, D.C.

As the House and Senate considered the Age Act amendments, researchers at the American Institutes for Research were conducting a study of retirement age policy, funded by the Ford Foundation and the Florence V. Burden Foundation. Harold Sheppard and Sara Rix produced a book reporting the results of their work entitled, *The Graying of Working America* (New York: Free Press, 1977). The study examined the economic, financial, and social ramifications of early retirement, later retirement, and projected population changes. The authors present projections concerning cost burdens of increasing numbers of nonworking older persons over the coming decades. The book also considers biomedical advances relating to mortality rates, effects of the energy and productivity issues on labor force participation, and the socioeconomic effects of early retirement. It is not a "how to" book for the businessman, but rather an informative and provocative discussion of these broad dimensions of the retirement age issue.

OLDER WORKERS AND RETIREMENT

In 1978 the Conference Board published a report, *Older Workers and Retirement*. Authored by Shirley H. Rhine, the publication reviews characteristics of older workers, age discrimination legislation, labor force participation rates and their implications, the older unemployed, and the pros and cons of mandatory retirement. It is a concise description of the circumstances in which retirement age ceilings are being lifted (New York: The Conference Board, 1978).

Also in 1978 the National Council on the Aging published the *Fact Book on Aging*. The book presents a profile of America's older population: demography, income, employment, health, housing, transportation, and criminal victimization. Authored by Charles Harris, the publication and its supporting research were financed by a grant from the Weyerhaeuser Foundation (NCOA, 1828 L Street, N.W., Washington, D.C., 1978).

The National Council on the Aging also published a study in 1975 on public perceptions of aging in America. *The Myth and Reality of Aging in America* was the report of a study conducted by Louis Harris and Associates, Inc., the pollsters.

HISTORICAL PERSPECTIVES ON
RETIREMENT AND AGING

Growing Old in America is a historical narrative by David Hackett Fischer, a social historian at Brandeis University. The book traces the changing attitudes of Americans toward older persons and the related changing experiences inherent in being old in America. Viewing the modern American scene in terms of a "youth cult" and old age as a "social problem" helps put light on the controversy that led to the end of mandatory retirement. Fischer holds that there is a swing back toward a more positive view of the aging segment of our population (New York: Oxford University Press, 1977).

Alex Comfort, best known for his book *The Joy of Sex* is actually a highly regarded gerontologist. A highly readable book written for the older person, entitled *A Good Age*, presents a wide range of insights into the characteristics, concerns, and anxieties of aging and retirement. His book illustrates the options open to people who wish to remain alert and active past middle age. "The urgent need is for 'old' people to learn to fight back against hogwash, classification, putdowns and rip-offs which, by virtue of the passage of time alone, society writes into the roles of people who could still be young" (New York: Crown Publishers, 1976).

An excellent discussion of retirement itself, based on a large survey of retirees, is presented in *Retirement in American Society*. The authors, Gordon Streib and Clement Schneider, examine reasons for retirement and attitudes regarding the retirement experience. It represents one of the most intensive studies of retirement conducted (Ithaca, New York: Cornell University, 1971).

AGING

Two books are noteworthy for those who wish to explore the state of our knowledge on aging and human development. Douglas Kimmel is author of a highly readable textbook entitled *Adulthood and Aging*. The scope covers the total life span, placing aging and retirement in context. Case illustrations are provided (New York: John Wiley & Sons, 1974). The other recommended book is *Prolongevity* by Albert Rosenfeld (New York: Knopf, 1976). This book reports on the advances of science in extending the life span and the social implications should the results have widespread effect. It is a well-documented and provocative book. Rosenfeld is Science Editor for *Saturday Review* and was previously Science Editor of *Life*.

RETIREMENT PREPARATION

The best available overview on the subject of retirement preparation is a report published by The Conference Board in 1977. The report, *Retirement: Reward or Rejection* highlights the issues addressed in this book and presents the results of a 1974 survey of 800 companies regarding retirement assistance provided to employees (O'Meara, 1977).

Many books have been published as guidebooks for retirement preparation. In addition to the many tools available from the AARP and other organizations, books aimed at the individual retirees have proliferated. One popular guidebook, by Elmer Otte, provides exercises, advice, and an excellent bibliography of pertinent articles and books. The *Re-*

tirement Rehearsal Guidebook is a good starting point in exploring this area of activity (Pictorial, Inc., 8081 Zionsville Road, Indianapolis, Indiana 46268, 1974).

HUMAN RESOURCE MANAGEMENT TECHNIQUES

A central focus of this book has been on the actions that will need to be taken by employers to implement more flexible retirement practices. There are many books and articles describing alternate approaches and specific techniques in human resource management. Because references were provided on specific topics in the chapters, references are not recommended here.

However, for the manager who wishes to explore the scope and depth of the field, an excellent starting point would be a perusal of the *Handbook of Personnel and Industrial Relations*. The Handbook, actually a series of eight paperback volumes, ultimately to be published as a single hardback volume, comprises commissioned papers on a wide range of human resource topics. Edited by Dale Yoder and Herbert G. Heneman, Jr., the handbook is the official publication of the American Society of Personnel Administration. Each chapter provides references which can lead the reader to other sources of information (Washington, D.C.: Bureau of National Affairs, 1974–1978).

Finally, a quarterly journal entitled *Aging and Work: A Journal on Age, Work and Retirement* is a useful periodic reference on topics pertaining to this book. Formerly *Industrial Gerontology*, the journal is published by the National Council on the Aging.

REFERENCES

Alpert, Helen, "Ten Secrets for Successful Retirement," *Retirement Living* (January 1973).

Anderson, Alan, Jr., " 'Old' is not a Four-Letter Word," *Across the Board* Vol. 15, No. 5 (May 1978), 20–27.

Atchley, Robert C., *Social Forces in Later Life: An Introduction to Social Gerontology* (Belmont, Calif.: Wadsworth, 1972).

Baltes, Paul B. and K. Warner Schaie, "The Myth of the Twilight Years," *Psychology Today* (March 1974), 35–40.

Barfield, Richard and James Morgan, *Early Retirement, the Decision and the Experience* (Ann Arbor: University of Michigan Survey Research Center, 1969).

Barkin, Solomon, "Retraining and Job Design: Positive Approaches to the Continued Employment of Older Persons," in *Industrial Gerontology*, Harold Sheppard (Ed.) (Cambridge, Mass.: Schenkman, 1970, 17–30).

Bartlett, Douglas M., "Retirement Counseling: Making Sure Employees Aren't Dropouts," *Personnel* (November-December 1974), 26–35.

Basnight, Thomas and Benjamin W. Wolkinson, "Evaluating Managerial Performance: Is Your Appraisal System Legal?" *Employee Relations Law Journal* Vol. 3, No. 2 (Autumn 1977), 240–254.

Baugher, Daniel M., "Age-Related Changes in Psychological Processes and Mandatory Retirement: Is the Older Worker Inherently Incompetent," unpublished manuscript, 1977.

Bengtson, Vern L., *The Social Psychology of Aging* (Indianapolis: Bobbs-Merrill, 1973).

Berlin, P. E., "Young Tigers and Other Corporate Jungle Inhabitants: Survival of the Fittest on Reduced Budgets," *Employee Relations Law Journal* Vol. 2, No. 3 (Autumn 1976), 172–187.

Binstock, Robert H. and Ethel Shanas (Eds.), *Handbook of Aging and the Social Sciences* (New York: Van Nostrand Reinhold, 1977).

Birren, James E. and K. Warner Schaie (Eds.), *Handbook of the Psychology of Aging* (New York: Van Nostrand Reinhold, 1977).

Bratthall, Kenneth, "Flexible Retirement and the New Swedish Partial Pension Scheme," *Industrial Gerontology* Vol. 3, No. 3 (Summer 1976), 157–167.

Britton, P. G. and R. D. Savage, "The MMPI and the Aged," *British Journal of Psychiatry* Vol. 112 (1965), 941–943.

Burger, Chester, *Creative Firing* (Toronto: Litton Educational Publishing, 1972).

Butler, Robert N., *Why Survive? Being Old in America* (New York: Harper and Row, 1975).

Butler, Robert N. and Myrna I. Lewis, *Aging and Mental Health: Positive Psychosocial Approaches* (St. Louis: Mosby, 1973).

Campbell, David P., *If You Don't Know Where You're Going, You'll Probably End Up Somewhere Else* (Niles, Ill.: Argus Communications, 1976).

Cavan, R., "Self and Role in Adjustment During Old Age," in *Human Behavior and Social Processes: An Interactionist Approach*, A. M. Rose (Ed.) (Boston: Houghton-Mifflin, 1962).

Cheedle, W. M., Fred Luthans, and Robert Otteman, "A New Breakthrough for Performance Appraisal," *Business Horizons* (August 1976).

Comfort, Alex, *A Good Age* (New York: Crown, 1976).

Cooper, K. H., *The New Aerobics* (New York: M. Evans, 1970).

Cumming, E. and W. Henry, *Growing Old: The Process of Disengagement* (New York: Basic Books, 1961).

Detman, Art, "The Trauma of Retirement" (An Interview with Dr. Arthur Schwartz), *Dun's Review* (October 1974), 19–32.

Eisdorfer, Carl and M. Powell Lawton, *The Psychology of Adult Development and Aging* (Washington, D.C.: The American Psychological Association, 1973).

Erikson, Erik, *Identity: Youth and Crisis* (New York: Norton, 1968).

Finch, Caleb E. and Leonard Hayflick (Eds.), *Handbook of the Biology of Aging* (New York: Van Nostrand Reinhold, 1977).

Fischer, David Hackett, *Growing Old in America* (New York: Oxford University Press, 1977).

Glamser, Francis D., "Determinants of a Positive Attitude Toward Retirement," *Journal of Gerontology* Vol. 31, No. 1 (1976), 104–107.

"The Graying of America," *Newsweek* Vol. 89 (February 28, 1977), 50–62.

Greene, M. R., H. C. Pyron, U. V. Manion, and H. Winklevoss, "Early Retirement of Industrial Workers and its Impact on Employment and Psychological Adjustment," University of Oregon, 1969. A Research Report sponsored by the Administration on Aging, Department of Health, Education, and Welfare.

————, "Personnel Policy, Retirement Adjustment, and Old Age," University of Oregon, 1969.

"The Growing Trend to Early Retirement," *Business Week* (October 7, 1972), 74–76.

Hall, Douglas T., *Careers in Organizations* (Pacific Palisades, Ca.: Goodyear Publishing, 1976).

Hall, Douglas T. and Khalil Nougaim, "A Examination of Maslow's Need Hierarchy in an Organizational Setting," *Organizational Behavior and Human Performance*, Vol. 3 (1968), 12–35.

Harris, Louis and Associates, *The Myth and Reality of Aging in America* (Washington, D.C.: The National Council on the Aging, 1975).

Harris, Charles S., *Fact Book on Aging: A Profile of America's Older Population* (Washington, D.C.: National Council on the Aging, 1978).

Hausman, L. J., O. et al., *Equal Rights and Industrial Relations* (Madison, Wis.: Industrial Relations Research Association, 1977).

Havighurst, R., B. L. Neugarten, and S. S. Tobin, "Disengagement and Patterns of Aging," in B. L. Neugarten (Ed.), *Middle Age and Aging* (Chicago: University of Chicago Press, 1968), 141–172.

Holley, William H. and Hubert S. Feild, Jr., "The Design of a Retirement Preparation Program," *Personnel Journal* (July 1975), 527–535.

Horvath, S. M. and E. C. Horvath, *The Harvard Fatigue Laboratory* (Englewood Cliffs, N.J.: Prentice-Hall, 1973).

Hunter, Woodrow, "Background Considerations for Research

Planning in Pre-Retirement Education" (Ann Arbor: unpublished manuscript, 1962).

Ingraham, Mark H., *My Purpose Holds: Reactions and Experiences in Retirement of TIAA-CREF Annuitants* (New York: TIAA-CREF, 1974).

Johnson, M. J. "Is 65+ Old?" *Social Policy* Vol. 7 (1976), 9–12.

Kasschau, Patricia L., "Reevaluating the Need for Retirement Preparation Programs," *Industrial Gerontology* (Winter 1974), 42–55.

Kimmel, Douglas C., *Adulthood and Aging: An Interdisciplinary, Developmental View* (New York: Wiley, 1974).

Kimmel, Douglas C., Karl F. Price, and J. W. Walker, "Retirement Timing and Retirement Satisfaction," (New York: unpublished manuscript, 1977).

———, "Retirement Choice and Retirement Satisfaction," *Journal of Gerontology* (in press, 1978).

Kinzel, Robert, "Resolving Executives' Early Retirement Problems," *Personnel* (May-June 1974), 55–63.

Koyl, Leon, "Technique for Measuring Functional Criteria in Placement and Retirement Practices," in H. L. Sheppard (Ed.), *Industrial Gerontology* (Cambridge, Mass.: Schenkman, 1970), 148–156.

Kuypers, J. A. and V. L. Bengtson, "Competence and Social Breakdown: A Social-psychological View of Aging," *Human Development* Vol. 16, No. 2 (1973), 37–49.

Laufer, Arthur C. and William M. Fowler, Jr., "Work Potential of the Aging," *Personnel Administration* (March-April 1971), 20–25.

Lazer, Robert I., "The 'Discrimination' Danger in Performance Appraisal," *Conference Board Record* (March 1976).

Lazer, Robert I. and Walter S. Wikstrom, *Appraising Managerial Performance: Current Practices and Future Directions* (New York: The Conference Board, 1977).

Levinson, Daniel *et al. The Seasons of a Man's Life* (New York: Knopf, 1978).

Levinson, Harry, "Appraisal of What Performance," *Harvard Business Review* (July-August 1976), 30–36.

Ludlow, Hope T., "Thinking About Retirement: Do We Know How?," *Conference Board Record* (August 1973), 48–62.

Manion, U. Vincent, "Why Employees Retire Early," *Personnel Journal* (March 1972), 183–207.

McCormick, Ernest J., "Job and Task Analysis," Chapter 15 in *The Handbook of Industrial and Organizational Psychology*, M. D. Dunnette (Ed.) (Chicago: Rand McNally, 1976), 651–696.

McFarland, Ross A., "The Role of Functional versus Chronological Age Concepts in the Employment of Older Workers," Unpublished paper presented at The Future of Retirement Age Policy Conference, American Institutes for Research, 1976.

Mechanic, D., *Medical Sociology* (New York: Free Press, 1968).

Meyers, D. and L. Abrahamson, "Firing with Finesse: A Rationale for Outplacement," *Personnel Journal* (August 1975), 432–437.

Meyer, Mitchell and Harland Fox, *Early Retirement Programs* (New York: The Conference Board, 1971).

Miller, D. C. and William H. Form, *Industrial Sociology* (New York: McGraw-Hill, 1951).

Mintzberg, Henry, *The Nature of Managerial Work* (New York: Harper & Row, 1973).

Mulanaphy, James M., *1972–1973 Survey of Retired TIAA-CREF Annuitants* Statistical Report (New York: TIAA-CREF, 1974).

Nekvasil, Charles A., "Without Mandatory Retirement: Then What?" *TWA Ambassador* (March 1978), 20–47.

Neugarten, Bernice L., "Age Groups in American Society and the Rise of the Young-Old," *Annals Amer. Acad.*, 1974 (September), 187–198.

Neugarten, B. L., Havighurst, R. J., and Tobin, S. S., "Personality and Patterns of Aging," in Neugarten, *Middle Age and Aging* (Chicago: University of Chicago Press, 1968).

Oberg, Winston, "Make Performance Appraisal Relevant," *Harvard Business Review* Vol. 50, No. 1 (January-February 1972), 61–66.

O'Meara, J. Roger, *Retirement: Reward or Rejection* (New York: The Conference Board, 1977).

———, "Retirement: The Eighth Age of Man," *Conference Board Record* (October 1974), 59–64.

————, "Retirement," *Across the Board* (January 1977), 4–9.

Orbach, Harold I., *Trends in Early Retirement* (Ann Arbor: University of Michigan–Wayne State University Institute of Gerontology, 1969).

Otte, Elmer, *Retirement Rehearsal Guidebook* (Indianapolis: Pictorial, Inc., 1974).

Owen, Roger (Ed.), *Middle Age* (London: British Broadcasting Corp., 1967).

Patz, Alan, "Performance Appraisal: Useful but Still Resisted," *Harvard Business Review,* Vol. 54, No. 3 (May–June, 1975), 74–80.

Perham, John, "Financial Counseling: Now It's the Top Perk," *Dun's Review* (July 1973), 37–40.

Pinto, Patrick R. and James W. Walker, "What Do Training and Development Professionals Really Do?" *Training and Development Journal* (July 1978).

Pollman, A. William, "Early Retirement: A Comparison of Poor Health to Other Retirement Factors," *Journal of Gerontology* Vol. 26, No. 41 (January 1971).

Prentice-Hall, "P-H/ASPA Survey: Pre-Retirement Planning Programs on the Upswing," *Personnel Management Policies and Practices Report Bulletin* Vol. 23, No. 25 (May 21, 1976).

Prentis, Richard S., "Who Helps the Retiree Retire?" *Pension World* (December 1975), 52–56.

Prien, Eric and W. W. Ronan, "Job Analysis: A Review of Research Findings," *Personnel Psychology* Vol. 24 (1971), 371–396.

Reichard, S., R. Levin and P. G. Peterson, *Aging and Personality* (New York: Wiley, 1962).

Rhine, Shirley H., *Older Workers and Retirement* (New York: The Conference Board, 1978).

Rosenfeld, Albert, *Prolongevity* (New York: Knopf, 1976).

Rosow, I., *Socialization to Old Age* (Berkeley: University of California Press, 1973).

Savage, R. D., "Old Age," in H. J. Eysenik (Ed.), *Handbook of Abnormal Psychology,* second edition (London: Pitmans, 1972).

Schlei, Barbara L. and Paul Grossman, *Employment Discrimination Law* (Washington, D.C.: BNA, Inc., 1976).

Schultz, James H., "The Economics of Mandatory Retirement," *Industrial Gerontology* Vol. 1, No. 1 (Winter 1974), 1–10.

Select Committee on Aging, 95th Congress, *Mandatory Retirement: The Social and Human Cost of Enforced Idleness* (Washington, D.C.: U.S. Government Printing Office, 1977).

Shapiro, H. D., "Do Not Go Gently," *New York Times Magazine* (February 2, 1977), 41–45.

Sheehy, Gail, *Passages: Predictable Crises of Adult Life* (New York: Dutton, 1976).

Sheppard, Harold (Ed.), *Industrial Gerontology* (Cambridge, Mass.: Schenkman, 1970).

Sheppard, Harold and Sara E. Rix, *The Graying of Working America: The Coming Crisis of Retirement Age Policy* (New York: Free Press, 1977).

Sheppard, Harold L., "Work and Retirement," in R. H. Binstock and Ethel Shanas (Eds.), *Handbook of Aging and the Social Sciences* (New York: Van Nostrand Reinhold, 1977), 286–309.

Skinner, John H. and Daniel A. Quirk, *The Impact of Age and Physical Ability on Employment* (Washington, D.C.: National Council on the Aging, 1973).

Smedley, Lawrence T., "The Patterns of Early Retirement," *AFL-CIO Federationist* (January 1974), 1–6.

Smith, P., Kendall, L. Hulin, C., *The Measurement of Satisfaction in Work and Retirement* (Chicago: Rand-McNally, 1969).

Streib, Gordon F. and Clement J. Schneider, *Retirement in American Society: Impact and Process* (Ithaca: Cornell University Press, 1971).

Super, Donald, *The Psychology of Careers* (New York: Harper and Row, 1957).

Sweet, Donald H., *Decruitment: A Guide for Managers* (Reading, Mass.: Addison-Wesley Publishing Company, 1975).

Teague, Burton W., "Financial Counseling for Top Executives," *Conference Board Record* (July 1973), 62–64.

Thompson, Paul H. and G. W. Dalton, "Performance Appraisal: Managers Beware," *Harvard Business Review* Vol. 48, No. 1 (January-February 1970), 149–157.

Thompson, W. E., "Pre-Retirement Anticipation and Adjustment in Retirement," *Journal of Social Issues* Vol. 14 (1958), 35–45.

Timiras, P. S., *Developmental Psychology and Aging* (New York: Macmillan, 1972).

Towers, Perrin, Forster & Crosby, *Early Retirement for Executives: Practices, Attitudes, and Trends* (New York: TPF&C, 1974).

———, *Mandatory Retirement: End of an Era?* (New York: TPF&C, 1977).

U.S. Bureau of the Census, *Current Population Reports* Series P-25, No. 601 (October 1975).

Walker, James W., "Individual Career Planning: Managerial Help for Subordinates," *Business Horizons* (February 1973).

———, "The New Appeal of Early Retirement," *Business Horizons* (June 1975), 43–48.

———, "Will Early Retirement Retire Early?" *Management Review* (January-February 1976a), 33–39.

———, "Let's Get Realistic About Career Paths," *Human Resource Management* (Fall 1976b), 2–7.

———, "Personal and Career Development," in Dale Yoder and H. G. Heneman, Jr. (Eds.), *ASPA Handbook of Personnel and Industrial Relations,* Volume 5 (Washington, D.C.: Bureau of National Affairs, 1977a), 57–74.

———, "Why Stop at 65?" *Management Review* (August 1977b).

———, "Does Career Planning Rock the Boat?" *Human Resource Management* (Spring 1978), 2–7.

Walker, James W. and Karl F. Price, "The Impact of Vesting, Early Retirement, Rising Cost of Living and Other Factors on Projected Retirement Patterns: A Manpower Planning Model," *Industrial Gerontology* Vol. 1, No. 3 (Summer 1974), 35–48.

———, "Retirement Policy Formulation: A Systems Perspective," *Personnel Review* Vol. 5, No. 1 (Winter 1976).

Walker, James W., Karl F. Price, and Douglas C. Kimmel, "Retirement Style and Retirement Satisfaction," paper presented at the Western Regional Conference, American Institute of Decision Sciences, San Diego, California (1978).

Wikstrom, Walter S., *The Productive Retirement Years of Former Managers* (New York: The Conference Board, 1978).

Wilson, Michael, *Job Analysis for Human Resource Management,* Manpower Research Monograph No. 36 (Washington, D.C.: U.S. Department of Labor, 1974).

Winter, R. E., "To Tighten Operations, Firms Force Men in 50's and 60's to Retire Early," *Wall Street Journal* (March 15, 1972).

Woodring, Paul, "Why Sixty-Five?" *Saturday Review* (August 7, 1976).

Woodruff, Diana S. and James E. Birren, *Aging: Scientific Perspectives and Social Issues* (New York: Van Nostrand, 1975).

SUBJECT INDEX

NAME INDEX